Daddy Cool

Daddy Cool

FINDING MY FATHER, THE SINGER
WHO SWAPPED HOLLYWOOD FAME
FOR HOME IN AUSTRALIA

DARLEEN BUNGEY

ALLEN&UNWIN

SYDNEY · MELBOURNE · AUCKLAND · LONDON

Allen & Unwin
83 Alexander Street
Crows Nest NSW 2065
Australia
Phone: (61 2) 8425 0100
Email: info@allenandunwin.com
Web: www.allenandunwin.com

A catalogue record for this book is available from the National Library of Australia

ISBN 978 1 76052 967 3

Set in 11.5/18 pt Sabon by Midland Typesetters, Australia
Printed and bound in Australia by Griffin Press, part of Ovato

10 9 8 7 6 5 4 3 2 1

The paper in this book is FSC® certified. FSC® promotes environmentally responsible, socially beneficial and economically viable management of the world's forests.

To Sam and Cassie

Pass it on

'Who in the world am I? Ah, that's the great puzzle.'

Lewis Carroll, *Alice in Wonderland*

Prologue

HIS TWO AUSTRALIAN DAUGHTERS carried him across the broad sands towards the headland that rises sharply from the last northern beach in the city of Sydney. Sun sparked off the lighthouse at the top of the scrubby rise. Giant boulders, elemental, lay at the base of the cliff on a rocky bed that spilled into the sea.

We were young enough then, in 1994, to easily negotiate the long haul over the tricky wet passage of stones leading to one of the most magnificent boulders. It would be his headstone and our farewell point to the man with several names. In his first life: Robert Ahern Cutter—Buster, Bob. And in his second: Lawrence Brooks—Lawrie.

Surrounding us were ancient rock engravings and burial sites once created by the Guringai people. Tens of thousands of years later, a Customs House had been built. In the 1800s, this area had been a bushrangers' hideout, a place for smugglers of sly grog. On this day, my sister brought a bottle of whiskey, our father's favoured spirit. It would be our toast to him.

In a beach suburb several kilometres away, his wife had no idea what was taking place. She knew no way of ever saying goodbye to the man she had loved for so long. When he had been cremated, and after the wake, our mother didn't— couldn't—discuss what might happen to her husband's ashes, to the remains of the man she had loved for almost half a century. And in the years that followed, she never asked.

High above the Tasman, the sea that merges into the Pacific, we cast him adrift. We imagined the ocean would carry him from his adopted home of Australia to his birthplace on the coast of California.

In the dust were the sights and sounds of him, particularly the sounds of him. His wonderful tenor's voice, a voice that could rise above all fault—clear, true, piercingly tender.

The deep bass of the ocean orchestrated his leaving. In an airy tumble, he briefly smudged the blue sky above and the white wash below. And then he was on his way. Eighty-seven years were dissolving, reforming . . . found, lost, then found again.

———

MY FATHER READ LIKE he sang.

Curled up in my bed, watching him turn the pages of *Alice in Wonderland*, his soft voice blanketed me. When he said, 'This is your first grown-up book', I grew like Alice, far larger than my room, swelling with pride that I had my father's undivided attention and, at my tender age of six, that he considered me an adult.

He was a wonderful reader. Words were important to him. He treated them like notes of music. Vowels and consonants were carefully articulated, each sentence perfectly pitched. Like a concert conductor, he drew action from the verbs, colour from the adjectives and guided the punctuation with precision—swift, slow, halt, stop.

Sitting next to me, reading aloud, he must have recognised Alice's plight: he knew how it felt to fall from one world into another, to change identity. Over the years, although infrequently, he would speak of that foreign past; but for the most part it lived in a deep tea chest stored indifferently on the sandy soil under the house where stone foundations supported the wooden bungalow.

In this crate his history tumbled. His handsome young face crumpled on crushed newspapers. His 78-rpm vinyl recordings warped in the heat. Paper mites censored his reviews. His publicity photographs slowly faded. And spiders continued to spin like a metaphor over this tangle of another time.

In his late thirties, he had married for the fourth and last time. At this midpoint in his life, he had shed a life of glamour and travel for a packed lunch, for a nine-to-five job. Occasionally, the names and places from his past—the singing venues of the 1930s—the Coconut Grove, the Royal Hawaiian Hotel, the St Francis Hotel, the Biltmore Bowl—would crop up in conversations, but a child pays meagre attention to such details. And while, in the 1950s, I wore my precious Mickey Mouse ears and looked longingly towards the USA as one big Disneyland, it held little sway with me that my father had once called it home.

Up until my mid-teens, he took singing engagements that fitted around his day job. The man who sang at the kitchen sink was the man who sang on the radio every week. The man who caught the train from a working-class suburb of Sydney to the Town Hall station was the man on his way to sing for the Queen. The man who stood in the living rooms of our neighbours' homes, singing in celebration of their anniversaries and birthdays, was the man I watched rise magically from the stage floor in the majestic State Theatre to sing alongside the organist. It was a double life that to me seemed normal. It wasn't until he was pictured leaning against a piano on the front page of the newspaper—the paper that he worked for as a proof-reader—that I realised he was different to any other father I knew.

In the years after his death, I began paying close attention to the lives of others. I wrote biographies of men who, not necessarily seeking fame, didn't shun it when it arrived: one rushed towards the spotlight, while the other backed into it. Although they were painters not performers, I began to question if it wasn't my father who was at the heart of my endeavours. Was he the man I had always needed to un-riddle? Not only the man who inexplicably reversed his life, but a father who could trouble as well as delight; a man my mother would at times ask me to understand, to forgive.

Finally, I decided the tea chest was my rabbit hole. Rather than never find the answers to my mysterious father, I chose to plunge in.

Chapter One

IN AN EARLY PHOTOGRAPH, black-and-white and stamp sized, I am six months old. I sit in a pram looking towards my father who, shirtless and wearing an old pair of trousers, sweats in the sun as he rakes grass seeds into a small patch of soil bordering the front of a just-built, two-bedroom semi-detached red-brick bungalow in Marrickville. I am watching the man who, in that year of 1948, had just been written up in *Tempo* magazine as a 'suave, sophisticated heart throb ... famous for his love songs'. The writer declared that, if Lawrie Brooks were to go to England, he would be 'a greater singer than England has ever produced'.

I have looked at that picture throughout my life and admired my father's labour, wondering at the high, old wicker pram I sit in and imagining my mother proudly pressing the button on the Box Brownie camera. But now, with the *Tempo* clipping in one hand and this photo in my other, I ask myself: why on God's earth wasn't he in England showing the Brits how it's done, instead of labouring over his mortgaged tablecloth-size lawn?

There are other images I carried from that house. The circular lampshade hanging above my cot with a red train travelling around it was comforting. But another memory was disturbing—it announced itself long before it appeared. Like distant thunder, the fearful noise grew until it was above my head—a plane descending, coming in to land at the neighbouring suburb of Mascot. It would send me into terrified tears and a toddling run. Like the story of Chicken Little, afraid of the sky falling in, I believed the great grey shadows across the sun were destined to come crashing down on top of me.

While I was researching this book, an earlier image of another powerful shadow revealed itself. On a high ridge, which looks eastward to the ocean and westward towards the city of Sydney, stands a concrete water tower, drum-shaped and elevated by pillars. I never understood why it had been as familiar to me as the Harbour Bridge or the ferries ploughing across the waters. I suspected that as a child I had seen it when my grandfather and I walked along the sea wall bordering New South Head Road, and sat on the steps leading down to the harbour. With the tower as a backdrop, we'd watch the flying boats—the Catalinas, great elephants with wings—take off and land at what was Australia's first international airport.

But it wasn't until I later found the house where my mother lived before her marriage that I finally understood the connection. Standing at the end of Black Street, Vaucluse, the water tower loomed large. With a shock of recognition, I understood that as a baby in arms and as a toddler I'd been in the street before, taken there to visit my grandparents while they still lived in the family home. To an adult that tower is imposing, but to my eyes then it must have been awesome—an enormous mountain in the landscape of memory.

Now I wonder what subliminal early images my father may have borne, what shadows were imprinted in his early memory that contributed to his restless ways? For a man who had never settled, the address in Marrickville of the first house he ever owned—9a Pilgrim Avenue—was aptly named. For nothing up to that point in his wandering life had been stable.

———

HE WAS CONCEIVED JUST as northern California collapsed into chaos; in April 1906, as San Francisco fell and burned in the great earthquake. His parents, Winthrop ('Winnie') and Louise, were shaken awake in the dark to a wild séance: timbers creaked, pictures flew off walls, furniture careered across the room, and the earth roared and cracked. San Jose, the Californian town known then as 'the prettiest place in the State', folded like a piece of origami.

From ruptured pipes, gas pooled towards fallen electrical lines. Through the darkness, the light from the fires that then erupted only hinted at the extent of the destruction. With sunrise, a ruined landscape swam out of the dust and smoke. Any building over two storeys had been levelled. As if Judgment Day had arrived and the Devil was the adjudicator, the Hall of Justice was destroyed. While most of the many churches were battered, the First Presbyterian Church and the Catholic Cathedral collapsed into complete ruin. Some kilometres away, inmates of the State Insane Asylum ran dazed and crying about the hospital grounds, while nurses and doctors and scores of fellow patients lay dead beneath the rubble.

In the aftermath, to put distance between themselves and San Francisco, my grandparents, Louise and Winnie moved almost 300 hundred kilometres south down the coast to Santa Maria, a small, predominantly farming town of around two thousand people.

But nature hadn't stopped throwing a tantrum. Just weeks before Robert Ahern Cutter made his entrance into the world, a January storm stalled over the Central Coast and the Lompoc Valley. It lasted four days. The Santa Maria River rose, dykes burst, bridges collapsed, railway lines were torn up and some sixteen hectares of crops washed away. These dramatic events set the scene for the hurly-burly of my father's young life to come.

He told me his first vivid memory was carrying a bucket full of eggs and delivering them unbroken. As the details of his early life reveal themselves, I begin to understand why this simple domestic scene would have been a precious moment in his young life. He would have held tight to the handle of that bucket because at last he could prove he was strong enough for the job. And he would have taken slow and careful steps because he'd seen how easily the eggs broke when his mother hit them on the side of the bowl. Successfully delivering the eggs meant that the black iron stove would soon warm the air, the air so often filled with cold voices, and then the house would be wrapped in the sweet scent of burning wood and the bread his mother baked.

His happy memories of these times were scant. His parents' marriage had been in trouble from the beginning. The twenty-six-year-old groom had taken a good time to walk his seventeen-year-old bride to the altar, for just five months later a strong, beautiful golden-haired boy was born. They named him Ronald. His death at the age of two was swift and never properly understood. 'Death by abdominal spasm' was all that the inept local Dr Brown offered.

Two weeks before burying her first son, Louise gave birth to her second, my father. He was a weak baby, not expected to survive. Once again the prognosis was stomach problems, and once again Dr Brown was flummoxed; nevertheless, he insisted she continue to breast feed throughout this period of trauma and grief. And so my father was nursed with tears. It wasn't until his third year, and a long line of doctors later, that he was pronounced sickly but safe.

——

MY FATHER SAID HE never forgot the sound, the way the notes bounced high and low. It was 'Alexander's Ragtime Band'. A man, walking down the road, had whistled the tune. It was happy. But then it wasn't, because that was the day his mother took him to his grandparents' house and he never slept in his own bed again.

It was a scandalous divorce case for the year 1912. Both his parents cited adultery. My great-grandfather John Conkey, attorney at law, represented his daughter, my grandmother Louise, in the Santa Barbara court. She asserted her husband Winnie had consorted with a prostitute in the house of ill repute of one Martha Dunlap in Santa Maria in 1911. Winnie, denying all charges of adultery with any woman, anywhere, countered with his own case in the hope of gaining custody of his son. He proposed that his wife had indulged in 'illicit and carnal intercourse with one Wallace MacDougall' over a two-month period in 1910, adding that these meetings took place in the marital home.

During the legal proceedings, although it was deleted from the final judgment papers, Louise admitted that she did have a liaison but stated that her husband had forgiven her at the time. Both alleged the other indulged in alcohol to excess, and both threw killing stones: Winnie calling his wife immoral and licentious, and Louise branding her husband dissolute and degenerate.

The weeks leading up to the court hearing must have been lonely and strange for Robert, full of whispers and silences. Then a day came that I imagine might have seemed to him like a Sunday. Everyone dressed in best clothes and they travelled to a place, quiet like a church, where a serious man behind a large table sounded like a minister.

The judge declared both the plaintiff and the defendant guilty of 'moral turpitude' (a phrase my father never forgot) and awarded custody of their son to his maternal grandparents. He was never to live with his parents again.

It is impossible to know what a child so young comprehends. I imagine the small boy standing at the epicentre of the confusion in that Santa Barbara courtroom, clinging tight to his grandmother's hand. In the last months of his life, with his stoicism strong but his powerful voice a whisper, all my aged father would allow of a wound that could never heal was, 'I was very upset.'

The divorce had been heralded by years of slow despair. Parenthood had been visited upon two people who, when illness and tragedy struck their first-born, had little idea of how to give support and comfort to each other.

My father had grown listening to his family's rhapsodic memories of his dead brother Ronald, whose absence crowded the house—a constant reminder of love lost. I vaguely remember passing references, but when you are young and running towards a future through treacle because days seem to stretch like years, the past is the last thing to hold your attention. I do remember him once proudly showing me a photograph of Ronald, a toddler with a sturdy little body and a halo of corkscrew blond curls.

In a letter written late in his life, my father disclosed that he was an inadequate replacement for such a bright vision. Like a steady drip, the constant reference to this ideal boy had eroded his confidence. He speaks of himself at a remove in this letter:

Dad, Mother, and Mother's parents had worshipped the beautiful and intelligently precocious Ronald. In fact, the repetition of Ronald's feats and antics gave young Bob a recognisable inferiority complex.

Winnie's nicknaming of his delicate son 'Buster' (a name that stuck until adulthood) would not have helped. My father laughed this off, saying, 'It was Winnie being ironic because I was anything but a bust 'em Buster.'

Perhaps the endless stories of his lost brother created, like my water tower, a shadow in my father's mind. Did Ronald become a perfectly formed mountain of a boy—monolithic, immovable—forever blocking out the light?

Chapter Two

LIKE MY FATHER, MY mother had been abandoned. She would never remember spending a day with her father, despite him living in the same city his entire life. This absent man (a grandfather I set eyes on only once) was an English immigrant who would create his own engineering business and make a small fortune in his adopted country.

Newly arrived in Australia, he roared into Boorowa, a small country town south-west of Sydney on his motorbike and, from under the noses of her horse-riding suitors, scooped up the beautiful Phyliss O'Brien and whisked her off to Sydney. He began an affair with another woman around the same time as my grandmother gave birth to a son, my mother's only sibling. In the year of my mother's birth, 1919, he deserted my grandmother, leaving her to fend for herself in a war-poor city—a woman with little formal education, with a toddler at her feet and my mother, Gloria, a newborn in her arms.

They survived with the help of family: Phyliss's Irish tribe gathered round. I remember some of them at the wakes. Mostly, I recall them from the point of view of plates overflowing with cakes and sandwiches, and frothy glasses of beer that passed over my head through the throng. Occasionally, a great-aunty or uncle, with names like Olga, Pansy or Curl, would notice me beneath the ruckus and stoop down to make a fuss or give me a shiny shilling.

Phyliss had the looks, the style and the charm to ensure that the grocer gave more than the food stamps allowed—an extra pound of butter here or half a dozen eggs there. And many a dinner date in fine restaurants resulted in a furtive slipping of fruit and bread and other comestibles into her handbag for the home table. Bravely, Phyliss got this job and that job, and they got by.

And then along came a young Dutch immigrant by the name of Jacobus Bosch, who delivered poetry and a proposal, and Gloria had a stepfather. In an attempt to fit in, as his surname was often judged to be German, he changed his name to Jay van Boss. My mother never spoke of her biological father who had deserted his family without a backward glance. She did once confide that, despite her stepfather being a most gentle and caring man, she believed the affection he showed her was second-hand—given only as a sign of his love for her mother. But life became lonelier still when Phyliss started drinking whiskey, which produced a Jekyll and Hyde effect. My mother could never bring friends home from school because she never knew which Phyliss might open the door.

During the Great Depression my mother's stepfather found work in various towns in the Northern Tablelands of New South Wales. They moved so regularly that, during my mother's early school years, the school inspector must have thought she was stalking him. Gloria was always there in one of his schools, with her hand in the air ready to provide an incorrect but inspired idea. One memorable time he asked: 'Why are ships referred to as she?' With no takers in the schoolroom, finally he nodded despairingly in my mother's direction, only to hear yet another of her non-curriculum answers: 'Because it takes a man to handle her.' The Ursuline Sisters in Armidale were not amused.

By the time Gloria arrived at the convent school in Bondi, despite the hardships of those tough financial times, life had assumed a more regular beat. But money was still so scarce that, to save the tram fare, my grandfather would often walk the eight or so kilometres to the city, where he was beginning to build a practice as a physical therapist.

One story I heard as a child illustrates this dire period when a third of the country was out of work. Edward, my mother's brother, described a scene in his school playground as a group of children gathered around watching a boy eating an apple. With hungry eyes they followed his every bite, until finally one boy made bold to ask: 'What's happening with the core? Can I have the core?' The snap reply: 'There ain't gunna be no core.'

In the convent school, my mother forged a lifetime bond. All through the years I remember a telephone call around Christmas time, either incoming or outgoing, between Gloria and a

Sister of Mercy who had once taught and cared for her. When her uniform needed mending, when her lunch wasn't adequate, whenever it became apparent that she didn't have whatever was required, even to the extent of a new school blazer, it was given to her with love and without fuss.

Light shines brightest through darkness and those kindnesses were never forgotten. Neither were the family gatherings. They'd sing rousing shanties and sad Irish laments, my grandfather's deep baritone shaking up the lyrics with his strong Dutch accent. When poetry was demanded, Phyliss would be on her feet, reciting from her extensive list. 'Laska', a passionate tale of doomed love and derring-do, was a favourite and a feat of memory, given the poem ran to two quarto pages.

And then the youngest, the star of the family shows, would be called upon. 'Come on Gloria,' they'd urge. 'Come on, make some fun!' And into the living room would arrive Abbott and Costello, or Jimmy Durante, or perhaps Greta Garbo. She would draw from a stable of Hollywood actors who were so carefully studied that every lisp or drawl, finger twirl or eye blink, was down pat.

If my mother couldn't be at the 'picture show', her ear would be pressed to the brocaded speaker on the front of the enormous mahogany home wireless set. With both parents working, when she arrived home from school the characters on the wireless became her other family. Her favourites changed with her age. Early on, there was Arthur Hahn, whose character 'Bimbo' managed to make children laugh during times when there wasn't much to laugh about. Then she moved on to children's serials and quiz shows and, from there, to a crooner by the name of Jack Davey.

When Davey started hosting a breakfast show, my mother heard that members of the live audience were invited to perform to win a cash prize. At the age of thirteen she got up in the semi-dark—the show went to air live at 7.30 a.m.—and set off by tram for the city in search of the radio station. By the time she found the studio, the broadcast was underway. 'I want to register for the prize, please,' she whispered. 'I do impressions.'

Someone signalled her towards the microphone and suddenly there she stood, a thirteen-year-old Zasu Pitts, all doleful eyes and wringing hands, delivering a perfect copy of the popular Hollywood comedienne's querulous, high-pitched voice. Completely lost in her alter ego she came to only when the studio audience erupted in applause. Then she watched, still dazed, as Jack Davey himself put ten shillings and sixpence into her winning hand, with the advice: 'You are very good. You should do something with your talent.'

The nuns on the other hand were doing their very best to discipline my mother into studious silence, continuously reprimanding the natural entertainer of the classroom with the catch cry: 'Gloria, you will never get a job talking.' I wonder at their reaction when, three years later, turning on the radio they heard my mother . . . talking, talking, talking.

She talked her way into a job at 2GB as assistant to the popular presenter, Goodie Reeve. Reeve had been a vaudeville performer, but with the birth of radio, like so many other stage entertainers, she stepped off the boards into the radio booth.

Reeve was a wonderful boss, kind and encouraging. My mother woke every day in a state of excitement, irritated that sleep had kept her from work. She would say to my sister and me as we grew up that she hoped we would find a job like hers, one that felt like you should be paying your employer.

In these early days, her hands were full, dealing with mail flowing like a wild river in response to Reeve's reading letters from listeners who had hit hard times. Pound notes fluttered out of the envelopes with an instruction 'Give this to the girl in trouble' or 'This five pounds is for the man being evicted' or 'Hope this covers the gas bill'. No receipts were asked for and most letters rarely signed.

One day, when my mother was manning the reception desk, a little old lady appeared, clutching one pound and ten pence in her gloved hand. 'For Mrs 'Obbs,' she said, thrusting it across to my mother. My mother refused the money, gently explaining that no help was required because Mrs 'Obbs was really Dan Agar acting in the popular radio serial. 'Oh, I know all that, dearie, but I feel so sorry for her . . . That Alfie shouldn't treat her like he does!' As the flowered hat bobbed off, its owner clutching her guinea, my mother was conflicted—she felt that somehow, by revealing the truth, she'd done the wrong thing.

Radio created a new dimension for so many lives. When my mother joined 2GB, it had only been a decade since the first public broadcast in Sydney. At the flick of a switch, lonely houses were filled with companionship. The housebound, including most married women in those days, were now delivered vital news, children's education programs, sports reporting, music, drama, comedy—in the 1930s and 1940s radio was TV and the internet combined.

Being smack bang in the centre of the most exciting medium of the time, in a period later dubbed 'The Golden Age of Radio', there is little wonder my mother was first at her desk every morning. She would be there to watch Jack Davey, the man known as 'Mr Radio', strolling in earlier than most. He had endless energy, planning his quiz shows, writing comedic themes and sharpening his presentation. His motto was: 'Bite off more than you can chew and chew like bloody mad.' His swift and naughty wit often landed him in trouble. Davey: 'All right, soldier; step up close to the microphone. What's your name and rank?' Soldier: 'Private Rubbing, sir.' Davey: 'Private Rubbing—that's not a name, that's a habit!'

Davey had studied memory training and was excellent at names; yet, despite this talent, when addressing my mother he seemed slightly confused by the name 'Gloria'. Until one day, about two months into her job, his face lit up. Pointing at her across a crowded room, he shouted, 'Good heavens, you're Zasu Pitts!' It had been three years since he'd pressed ten shillings and sixpence into her hand. Soon it was revealed how Davey on that day, with no prize money at the ready, had raced around cajoling the crew in the control booth to lend him a bob here and a bob there.

Back then, Davey said that my mother should do something with her talent and now he, together with Goodie Reeve and a host of other 2GB personalities, encouraged her to do so. The children's afternoon program was a free-for-all: anyone who could be roped in took part—from Davey to drama director Harry Dearth, to the pianist Jack Lumsdaine, to Goodie Reeve . . . and now sixteen-year-old Gloria van Boss.

Dearth, known and loved for his perfectionism, coached Gloria for her first part as a princess in a fairy story. Standing her at the end of the long office corridor, he made her 'project' (it was the first time she'd heard the word). He kept on and on until, just before her tears almost came, she heard the glorious words: 'Good girl.' There must have been a lovely innocence about my mother for all to see, for the parts that came her way were usually for the heroine, the Beauty to the Beast.

On air and off, entertainment among these creative people never stopped. It was a tight-knit group that observed each other closely and with affection. There was a Jack Davey joke involving my mother that sums it up for me. My mother grew into a woman with a figure that was slender, definitely not curvaceous, and so Davey quipped to the unit: Q: 'What's the definition of optimism?' A: 'Gloria tucking her hankie into the bodice of her frock.'

One day, when Harry Dearth, the producer of the children's program, became a father, the staff took him out to the Hotel Metropole to celebrate. With the company busy playing a practical joke on Dearth, only Davey made it back in time for the program. Rather than playing fill-in music, he played all the roles himself, jumping from one side of the microphone to the other, creating sound effects, hitting himself and groaning, while all the time attempting to change accents and the timbre of his voice. His efforts may have convinced some listeners but not Mr Horner, the general manager, who phoned through immediately, demanding to speak to the producer. Dearth was still locked in the toilet at the hotel and on release, after quelling his desire to murder his workmates, he was more than grateful Horner had a well-developed sense of humour.

Radio gave my mother the sense of freedom to set out on that Bondi tram and get up on that stage. Soon after, the family she found in the radio unit gave her confidence not only to be Zasu Pitts, but to be herself. Radio was central to my mother's life. As a girl, it was her company and tutor, later it was her employer, and then her matchmaker—responsible for ushering my father into her office at 2GB one fated day in the 1940s.

Chapter Three

MY FATHER GREW UP in the home of his maternal grandparents. John and Blanche Conkey believed the world turned on family and, in the years to come, their example would be his saving grace. John had been the youngest District Attorney for the county of Saratoga in the state of New York. But, in 1892, they sold the home they loved, left behind relatives and friends on the Eastern Seaboard and headed west for the sake of their eldest daughter, who had a suspected case of tuberculosis.

John found it hard to establish his law practice in San Jose, due in great part to his standing up against corrupt city bosses. Through this difficult period, Blanche helped support her husband by opening a fancy needlework shop and selling the lace she made. By 1905, John had become a resident of Santa Barbara and was admitted to the US circuit court. Back east, while studying for the bar, he had earned money by reporting for the *Saratoga Eagle*. After they moved to Santa Maria, an opportunity arose to purchase the local newspaper, *The Graphic*, and he took it.

There was always music in the house on Chapel Street. It was well known in the small town of Santa Maria that any musician, permanent or passing through, was welcome there. John had been raised in such a house. John's father, my great-great-grandfather, with the biblical name of Ithamar, had a voice of such quality that Jenny Lind, the 'Swedish Nightingale', while in New York City on her acclaimed American tour, insisted on singing duets only with him.

Apart from being a wonderful basso soloist and a recognised authority on oratorio singing, Ithamar was a gifted organist, the first at the Central Baptist Church in Norwich, Connecticut. Later, he built the organ at The Little Church Around the Corner in New York City and became resident organist there. Along the way, he composed *Rathbun*, a classic of American hymnals.

And so my great-grandfather, John, never knowing life without music, encouraged his own children's musical talent. At the age of twelve, his youngest daughter, my grandmother Louise, gave a cornet solo in San Francisco with one critic proclaiming her performance as 'veteran . . . every note coming clear and true'. She became part of a touring company of children known as 'The California Brownies', who travelled up and down the West Coast and to eleven other states. She was, according to one press blurb, one of the best-known child musicians in America. Another critic extolled her tones as 'pure . . . her mastery complete'.

All of John Conkey's children performed in public throughout their adult lives: Louise on cornet, her sister on piano and her brother on trombone. But John never heard a voice in his family that held the promise of his father, Ithamar—not until *my* father, his grandson, began to sing.

———

JOHN CONKEY WAS A dedicated Democrat. His fierce support for Woodrow Wilson, his organisational skills and his editorial column in *The Graphic*, all combined to win him appointment as Postmaster of Santa Maria. When the war broke out, he arranged for his grandson to be let go from school early each day to deliver daily telegrams and dispatches from the front.

After the town issued a declaration that all schools be closed due to an epidemic of the Spanish flu and made it illegal to hold any kind of group meetings, my father continued his job despite this invisible enemy entering Santa Maria. It was a force responsible for killing far more than the millions dying in the war in Europe.

The saloons on 'whiskey row' were closed; even those diehards had called it a day. The people still serving in the stores and banks wore white gauze masks, as did most citizens who didn't want a hundred-dollar fine. The Red Cross had given the masks out to everyone, but some kids just used them to carry marbles. There was a rhyme they chanted as they skipped rope:

I had a little bird
Its name was Enza
I opened the window
And in-flu-enza.

Digging a trench couldn't save you. This killer was more invisible than mustard gas and almost as fast as a bullet. You could be fine at dinner and dead by breakfast. The only medicines were lemon or warm malted milk. People died by the thousands. Blood frothed out of mouths and noses, or eyes haemorrhaged, or there was internal bleeding, and then death.

It must have been eerily quiet as Buster ran through the besieged town carrying news of destruction and death; so quiet he would have heard the stones kicking up on the dusty roads. So many people were dying that there weren't enough coffins or gravediggers to go around. In Santa Maria, funerals were limited to fifteen minutes. Bodies piled up high inside Dudley-Hoffman Mortuary. The white hearse drawn by a pair of horses draped in white crocheted shawls carried children. A black hearse signalled an adult corpse. Perhaps my father felt that at his age he didn't belong to either group and so how might they carry him to the grave? His brother had died. Why shouldn't he? The only official instructions to avoid the disease were to stay away from crowds, to cover your nose and mouth if anyone sneezed, and not to be scared. I imagine, as he ran, those words repeated with the rhythm of his footfall and the blood beat pounding in his ears: 'Don't be scared . . . don't be scared . . . don't be scared.'

On the eleventh hour of the eleventh day of the eleventh month, when the Germans were officially defeated and four years of carnage drew to a close, my father was eleven years old. But it wasn't until the summer of 1919 that peace was secured, the flu pandemic began to wane, and life started to return to normal.

As normal as it could be for a boy who had both parents, and a new stepfather and stepmother living in adjoining towns just up the coast.

For some years, during school vacation, he travelled to the small resort town of Pismo Beach, around 30 kilometres north of Santa Maria and reachable by the Pacific Coast railway. It must have been strange going between two different houses and two step-parents.

I have no idea why he didn't like Winnie's new partner. She had been a child actress called Baby Dodie and in adulthood she still went by the name Dodie. She must have been exceptionally unpleasant because never in my life do I remember my father using the word 'despised' at any time, for anyone, but that was the only description he ever gave of his feelings for her.

But he told me he liked Butch, his mother's new husband, who had been a butcher but now worked as a store-hand. This allowed him to practise his major occupation, that of boot-legger—he distilled whiskey and sold it under the counter during the dry years of Prohibition. They lived in a bungalow with a veranda and had two golden cocker spaniels, one named Rock and the other Rye. Butch was kind, giving Rye to my father to take home after one visit.

Pismo Beach stretched for 27 kilometres. Occasionally, there were car races along the sand, and horse and buggy drivers gathered to 'ooh' and 'aah' at the new machinery. A lot of people just sat around fully dressed on the sand and picnicked. But once you got past the tourists and the few shops and the dance pavilion built on stilts over the water and the 'tented city'—where people lived within walls of striped fabric with running water, electricity and laundry service laid on—you were alone with the sound of the seabirds and the dogs barking. It was a long walk out to the breakers if you wanted to get wet.

When he felt like a visitor in his parents' homes, he had the long free stretch of beach and the fresh salty air to fill his lungs. He knew when he returned to Chapel Street that he would be with the two people in the world who really knew him, and where he felt truly at home.

His grandparents, Blanche and John, were religious to the extent they observed church on Sunday, but the denomination never mattered to them. Nevertheless, he attended Sunday school at the Baptist Church for several years. He would wait six long days each week to see the heavenly blonde from Texas called Lorraine (he never forgot her name). No doubt it was this vision that inspired him to win a silver cup after a three-month-long competition in religious studies. To add to the inestimable trophy of impressing Miss Texas, he won yet another accolade—five dollars in prize money in an essay competition for expounding on why Santa Maria needed a new high school.

Entering the old high school he had good grades, but socially he flunked. It was a small town and the ragging and taunting in those first years was never shaken off—he was still called 'Rosy' (earned because of his pale skin and flushed cheeks in earlier years) and 'Buster'.

He excelled on another stage. His grandparents' house was always full of interesting people—political and theatrical, writers, musicians and composers. As a child, he was encouraged to learn music and perform at musical events and soirees, accompanied at various times by his aunt, mother, uncle and, in the early years, by his father. At the age of thirteen, he took a leading part in one of the biggest events ever staged in Santa Maria. Dressed as Uncle Sam, he led hundreds of schoolchildren, all clad in white and carrying flags, into the centre of the town. It was his voice that led the vast assemblage in the song 'America'. At fourteen, he performed one of his father's published songs in a musical revue at the Gaiety Theatre.

When Woodrow Wilson was no longer President, John Conkey was no longer Postmaster. On top of that, the circulation of *The Graphic* plummeted when its competitor, the *Santa Maria Times*, went from weekly to daily. However, at this time of financial struggle in many parts of the country, Orange County was thriving and, at the request of their daughter Bess and her husband, they agreed to help finance a paint store in Fullerton. Once again, John and Blanche sold up and moved house for the sake of family.

My father quaked at the idea of moving. The abandoned child clung to the familiar. At half his age, I had moved house four times. Sandwiched between my parents, I felt secure enough to go anywhere and didn't give our early nomadic life a second thought.

———

MY FATHER, IN HIS lifetime, performed live to well over a million people. But, at the age of fourteen, arriving at Fullerton High School mid-term and walking into a room full of new classmates, his nerves overwhelmed him. As he rounded the door to his introductory algebra class, he heard a yell: 'Hey there, good looking!' and then felt a blow to his ear. His reaction was to pick up the weapon, a heavy wooden-backed blackboard eraser, and return it with speed towards the laughing open face of his tormentor, wild Stanley Smith.

This was obviously the reply Stan was looking for because, after school that day, the two boys got chatting and within the week Buster was bouncing out of town on the handlebars of Stan's bicycle, towards the Smith ranch. 'That ranch . . .' he wistfully recalled, and then paused to add six words that stretched across the long, lonely years of his childhood '. . . I began to live that day.' Raised by elderly grandparents, the fragile, sidelined, unsure teenager, who shared a bedroom with his crabby middle-aged uncle, found himself in a boy's dream.

Stanley and his two brothers lived in a two-room bunkhouse next to the barn, far enough away from the main house and their parents and seven-year-old kid sister, Katharine, for Buster to feel intoxicated by the freedom. The boys had grown up in their own world, running barefoot through the irrigation mud. They picked oranges from the trees, Concord grapes from the vines strung off wires along the driveway, walnuts from the two trees by the main house and avocados from the tree on the edge of the front lawn.

There was no electricity, no postal service, no mains anything, but there must have seemed to be more air at the Smith ranch, for everything was writ large in those orange groves. In contrast to Buster's early memory of his mother scrubbing clothes on a hand-held washboard in a small tub in their tiny kitchen, the Smiths' weekly washday was alfresco and an all-day affair. Out in the backyard, they built a fire under a huge iron tub supported on two sides by brick walls. Cakes of soap cut into small pieces were thrown in the cauldron to melt. Then a sturdy wooden shovel, just over a metre long, stirred the clothes. Next the laundry was lifted, scalding hot and dripping with suds, onto a bench, then hoisted into huge galvanised tubs full of cold water, first one and then another, to be rinsed. Finally, the garments were passed through a hand-cranked sturdy wringer to be made ready for the washing line. It was operatic.

To my father's eye, Stan seemed to move under the glow of an arc lamp. His good-natured swagger came as naturally as his breath. Whatever Stan set about doing, no matter how dangerous, he could convince you it was worth the risk. His confidence was infectious and, although my father was still slight and uncertain of his physical skills, he was encouraged to take a run at things.

They had fun with boxing gloves. Stan taught him the moves and soon he became light on his feet and quick with the jabs. They went on climbing expeditions, and the boy who had grown up fearful of heights now, when he reached the peaks, happily dangled his feet on the edge of nothingness. Looking out over the never-ending of the great desert, out towards and beyond Death Valley, Buster's world expanded. Up to this point, swimming in the ocean had been a nervous occupation. But at Laguna Beach, between the natural pools formed by the coastal rocks, swimming with Harry by his side—Harry who, like his brother Stanley would do a high dive into a bucket—trepidation was replaced with joy.

Stan became the lost brother and Stanley's mother everything Buster's mother was not. Through the years, my father grew to believe that she was a woman who 'had the strength to mother all creation'. From her kitchen, he would be treated to velvety mashed potato and chicken, dusted in clouds of flour and fried in her huge black skillet, that would crunch and melt into his dreams. There were croquet games on the front lawn, four-handed poker with Stanley's father in the front parlour, and singing with the entire family to the popular tunes of the day played by Stan on the upright piano from his vast collection of sheet music.

By the time Stan turned sixteen, he had a part-time job at the Rialto movie theatre as ticket collector and usher, while his brother Harry worked as projectionist. The poker games were played later and in the bunkhouse. If the younger Leslie woke, one of them would read him back to sleep with a dime store Western and then, under the light of a kerosene lamp, they'd play on till early morning. The alarm would be the slamming of a screen door and Stanley's mother yelling from the back porch off the kitchen: 'Are you lazy loafers going to sleep all day?'

Stan, always ahead of the game, eventually introduced my father to Camel cigarettes and bootleg hooch. The 1920s were in full-throttle roar. Women had the vote and to celebrate their new freedom they shrugged off shrouding fabric and restrictive underwear, raised their hemlines and plunged their necklines. To further let their hair down, they bobbed it, and sex became a topic of general conversation.

In this heady time of change, the heavily eye-lined Rudolph Valentino, the great lover and adventurer of the silver screen, became the idol of the bunkhouse. In an effort to conjure him and his foreign ways, the boys lit small cones of incense. The sweet smoke swirled through the sparse wooden sleep-out and scented the air with the exotic, the unexplored—the endless possibilities that lay just beyond their adolescent grasp.

In later years, when my father took to the stage, when he himself became idolised, when he held vast audiences under his sway in buildings ten times larger than the Rialto, some of the applause would be owed to Stan and Harry, the boys from the bunkhouse who gave him that most precious commodity, confidence.

Both my parents lavished this gift on my sister and me. Throughout our lives there was never an achievement so insignificant that it wouldn't be met with praise, or an endeavour so small that it didn't merit their support and encouragement.

Chapter Four

AT TWENTY-TWO, TWENTY-FIVE CENTS changed the direction of my father's life. He was entranced. It wasn't that the figure on the screen was opening his mouth and words were coming out—on that count every person in the movie theatre was transfixed, for this was the first feature-length Hollywood 'talkie'. It was the electrifying one-way communication between Robert Cutter and the singer on the screen, Al Jolson.

He felt that Jolson was looking at him, singing only to him, showing him the way his life would be, outlining his destiny.

The opening black-and-white caption card of *The Jazz Singer* had all the fervour of a religious experience. It read: 'In every living soul, a spirit cries for expression—perhaps this plaintive, wailing song of Jazz is, after all, the misunderstood utterance of a prayer.' These words declared his conversion. He would be a singer.

When Al Jolson took to the boards and belted out 'Toot, Toot, Tootsie', he displayed all the on-stage confidence that, to this moment, my father had lacked.

Walking out of the dark cinema, inspired, the young man determined to try his luck. 'By Jesus,' he confirmed to his newfound self, 'I'm going to sing.'

He would shake off his shyness and at last follow the wishes of his musical family. He would become a singer who had the brio to say to his audience, as Jolson so famously did in this film: 'Wait a minute! Wait a minute! You ain't heard nothin' yet.'

Robert's voice had always held great promise. At fifteen, his Aunt Bess had arranged singing lessons. But despite his family pushing him towards a singing career, he had always shied away. It took Al Jolson to convince him to study seriously. He contacted a teacher, Frank Carroll Giffen, a tenor baritone with years of professional singing and teaching experience, who had toured as a concert singer throughout Europe and been a founder of the San Francisco Opera Company. Giffen taught singing to emerging movie stars at his studio in Hollywood and was impressed enough with the young man's talent and potential to offer him, as a gift, five one-hour lessons.

Giffen became a mentor to my father. He gave him faith in his talent and encouraged a new religious belief, one that was becoming popular in Hollywood at the time. He recommended Christian Science as a way to allay physical fears, as a method to create an inner calm, and as a doctrine that would instil a sense of control.

It worked, ultimately revealing its success during a 60-kilometre an hour westerly wind. As a boy during vacations with his grandparents in Santa Barbara, and then in later years, my father had sailed with various crews. On this particular day, in a six-metre sloop helmed by a novice, the storm snatched up their boat off Newport Beach. As the skipper tried unsuccessfully to get past the partially wrecked breakwater into Balboa Bay, my father was acutely aware that this was a recent site of several lethal yachting accidents. In the treacherous moments before they successfully entered the bay, a realisation suddenly hit him: the fear of death had left him.

In June 1930, he competed in the Fourth National Radio Audition, sponsored by Atwater Kent, the radio manufacturer. From hundreds of hopefuls, Robert Cutter won the state finals for Orange County. Together with the other county winners, he was broadcast over radio station KHJ.

It was a huge country-wide competition and it held the state of California in thrall. He'd sung in public before, but the thrill of knowing his voice would be carried across the country must have been extraordinary.

My father couldn't have known that this was just the beginning—that over the years to come his voice would be broadcast many thousands of times: at home, in Europe, and over half a world away.

—

ROBERT CUTTER'S CAREER SOON hit a major obstacle, the Great Depression. By 1931, America was hungry and California crippled, with a quarter of the state unemployed. Through a family connection, he was working as a painter at the Evangeline, an enormous residence on West 6th Street, Los Angeles, run by the Salvation Army to provide affordable shelter for young women away from home and family. When he didn't have a paintbrush in his hand he was singing, looking for that one opportunity that could change everything.

In January, the month of his twenty-fourth birthday, his father came knocking at his door. Winnie was on his uppers: his permanent job gone and his long-term partner, Dodie, having left him. His early life had played out like a Boy's Own Adventure: a journey to the Yukon to search for gold, a run at professional State athletic events, a try at professional baseball and a stint as sports couch.

Winnie was gifted, possessing a wit that suited his surname and a talent not only for sport but for politics, literature and art. As a young man, he mixed with the poet George Sterling and writer Jack London, and his own poetry was published in *Overland* magazine, as were his editorial cartoons in *The Call* newspaper, which he quit because he 'wouldn't draw to orders'.

After the divorce from my grandmother, he relied on his skill as pit drummer, playing at the Elmo Theatre in San Luis Obispo, and composing music and poetry—occupations that didn't pay well or regularly. Towards the end of the great epidemic Winnie contracted influenza, which left him with a weakened heart. Having just turned forty, he threw away his pipe, alcohol and late nights with musicians and moved to Sacramento, taking a fresh-air job as a 'car man', a tram conductor. Working on the cable cars he regained his strength. At forty-two, he became a sports journalist on the *Sacramento Union*, but his strident opinions caused trouble. Writing under the name 'Win', he would allow disgruntled readers all the column inches required for their rants, declaring to one 'Disgusted Fan' who found him 'the most sarcastic of sports writers': 'I hope I never become so ossified in thought and action as not to preserve the open mind.'

Winnie's father and brother, both medical doctors, were dedicated to building a drug store, which would eventually become Cutter Laboratories, a multi-million-dollar pharmaceutical company. Perhaps Winnie had too many talents, but none of his family's sense of continuity and purpose rubbed off on him. His life was a continuous pole vault: a power-driven run at this or that, an inspired leap into the light, and then the come-down.

But his son adored him. When he spoke of him to me, it was always with a boyish pride, always exalting Winnie's various talents—giving heroic flesh to the shadow. The few summer vacations Buster spent at Winnie's house on L Street in Sacramento must have been precious. As a teenager he was able to take part in discussions with his father's friends—the musicians, writers, actors. I imagine that he felt the weight of his father's arm around his shoulders, heard the words 'my son' as he was pulled in close. I know they watched baseball in the best seats and the son saw his father, the celebrated sports writer, acknowledged by the coaches and the players, and even some of the spectators. Throughout his life it's a fair bet that every time my father tasted summer ripe cherries his thoughts flew to that house on L Street and the backyard where two large cherry trees flourished. Winnie's arrival in Los Angeles in 1931 bookended that time.

Robert convinced his boss to hire his fifty-four-year-old father as part of the painting crew at the Evangeline. By day, they worked side-by-side and spent evenings in each other's company in a rooming house on Garland Avenue, just blocks from the work site. Winnie revelled in the physical labour. He did his job so well he was deemed as good as two men. My father always boasted that the foreman said, 'Give me another like your father and we'll finish the job early.'

Yet, the man once hailed as 'the greatest all-round athlete on the Pacific Coast', who had been playing the physically testing game of gridiron seven years before, was suddenly felled. Winnie had contracted syphilis. In that era, before penicillin, syphilis affected up to ten per cent of all US adults at some point in their lives. Government-sponsored poster campaigns cajoled and scared the populace into constant vigilance and regular blood tests. The doctors had declared Winnie cured but perhaps this disease, coupled with the damage inflicted by influenza, had weakened his athletic heart. Just before dawn on 3 July 1931, in the Los Angeles County General Hospital, six days after suffering a stroke, he died. Watching that firebrand of physical fitness bedbound and broken was terrible but losing his father just as they had found each other was doubly cruel. There must have been some comfort in knowing Winnie had witnessed his son's fortunes about to change.

———

THE FIRST INTERESTING TURN of events came that February, when Robert Cutter and Professor Albert Einstein received equal billing on the front page of the *LA Examiner.*

The physicist had been in California visiting the prestigious Zoellner Conservatory of Music and playing a little Beethoven and Mozart on his violin. Inspired by the proximity of the great man, my father put down his paintbrush, picked up a pen and composed a song titled 'Now: The Ein-stein Song'—distilling the notion of relativity with lines like:

Yesterday is done, tomorrow will not come . . .
we'll never worry over what's to come,
or what's undone
for you see that it makes the sum: Now.
We'll drink to Now—to good old Now. It's always: Now.

When the radio programmers insisted they needed the professor's approval before broadcasting the song, my father duly wrote to Einstein. He received, to his delight, a handwritten reply in the form of a rhyming couplet in colloquial German:

Et was blod! Dooh meinetwagen—Ich furwahr hab nichtchts dagegan!

Loosely translated:

Though somewhat silly I don't mind.
There's no objection I can find.

Inspiring Einstein to poetry was an unusual turn of events for a young house-painter, but it wouldn't be Robert Cutter's last connection with the Zoellner Conservatory. In the first half of 1931, through his association with Giffen Studios, he began taking part in various Hollywood concerts and competitions. In June, a letter arrived from Joseph Zoellner Jr:

It gives me pleasure to write you that unanimously the judges awarded you a six week scholarship with Hardesty Johnson [a renowned tenor who had been a faculty member of the Juilliard School]. Congratulations on your fine ability. Wishing you every success, which you surely will have.

Just one week later, hard on the heels of this great news, came Winnie's fatal stroke. That day, in a car lent by his foreman, the grieving son drove to Fullerton. The familiar roads must have seemed foreign; the happy people, bustling about as they prepared for their July Fourth celebrations, like beings from another planet.

It was only when he walked into his grandparents' arms that the world pulled focus. Sleeping under their roof repaired him. The following day he went looking for his old school friend Stanley Smith.

Chapter Five

'LOVE AND MARRIAGE'. Around the time my father was singing this song on the ABC's (Australian Broadcasting Commission) Hit Parade in 1956, my classmates and I were peering out of school windows and around playground walls at the only attractive young nun in the convent, and the only handsome young priest in the presbytery. Unbeknown to Héloïse and Abélard, we would giggle and gossip and serenade them . . . 'Love and marriage' . . . from behind the curtain of our hands. Even in our cruel innocence we understood enough to notice whenever they met how happy the priest's face became, and how animated our dour teacher suddenly appeared.

At home, I also had sufficient antennae to note that whenever my father's past was mentioned my mother shut down the conversation. Divorce carried a stigma in the 1950s, particularly in our neck of the woods, among the church-going women who walked their children to and from the convent school just a handful of houses away on the crest of a hill. They'd lean over the fence, chatting, careful not to bruise the petals of my mother's prized chrysanthemums. I'm not sure just what she told them then, but years later she would tell me: 'Don't worry about being the first, just make sure you're the last.' At the time all my mother would allow was: 'Your father married his high school sweetheart.' There was never any expansion on that, or mention of the parade of women and wives who came after.

—

TWENTY-FIVE YEARS BEFORE I was running around the school playground singing silly songs, my grieving father was looking to find his friend Stanley Smith, with not the slightest idea he would find a wife instead. The only people he found home at the ranch that fated day were Stanley's little brother, Leslie, and his sister, Katharine.

He had known Katharine since she was five, and through all those years she would be constantly thrown out of the bunkhouse. Now here she stood—a soon-to-be divorced nineteen-year-old, with almond-shaped blue eyes, luminous skin and wavy blonde hair. More desirable than any woman he'd ever seen. He had observed her as she entered her teens; he had listened to her at thirteen playing 'Enticement' on Stan's piano and, as she grew up, he had become intrigued by her impish ways, watching as she became even more brashly 'with it' than Stan.

On this day the lonely threesome—Leslie without his older brothers, Katharine casting off a husband, and a fatherless young man—headed out to forget their unhappiness. From the passenger seat, my father gazed in fascination at Katharine's unselfconscious, don't-give-a-damn, freewheeling attitude as she drove the old family car—the Paige—just like her brothers, as if she owned the world.

Picking up a couple of bottles of moonshine (Prohibition still in force) and several packets of Camels, they headed to one of the busiest dance spots on the coast, 'Rendezvous Balboa', down at Balboa Beach. To speed them on their way they drank the booze neat.

The Fourth of July fireworks painting the night sky over the ocean seemed arranged just for them. There was a dance floor and the insistent rhythm of the band. With her arms around him and his guiding her, this girl represented a place that held some of the happiest memories of his life. All their shyness stripped away by the alcohol, they left the dance floor, still locked together, drifting away from the electric lights towards the stretch of beach under moonlight.

Soon all they saw and heard were the occasional bursts of colour shimmering across the sky, the faraway dance music and the rolling sea. Then there was only the perfume of her and the ocean salt, only the softness of her against the sand, and the kisses . . . and the kisses . . . and the night folding into a place far away from hurt and sadness.

But, too soon, the hand of the law reached down and grabbed the lover by the collar. Drunkenness on weekends and public holidays contributed in no small way to the council's civic revenue. So the rest of that night was spent not with

Katharine, but in the Balboa lock-up. He begged his jailers to let him speak to his old sailing buddy and friend of his grandfather, the District Attorney for Orange County, Sam Collins. But that request, coming from a three-sheets-to-the-wind beach-loiterer, wasn't taken seriously and dismissed with: 'Everybody wants to speak to Sam Collins.'

It took the hefty sum of twenty-five dollars (around a basic weekly wage) to set him free the following morning. Once out of the lock-up, and still under the influence of the intoxicating brew of death and sex, he made straight for the ranch to tell Katharine he wanted to marry her.

When Katharine's parents, Will and Lenore, got to hear of the romance, they were furious. Will's response was to threaten to bust Robert's nose: 'Sleeping out there in the bunkhouse with my boys, and having it off with their sister.'

The Smiths had allowed their fifteen-year-old daughter to marry a man almost twenty years older; and, having agreed, no doubt they wanted the marriage to last. Captain Richard Steven George Shipley III came with credentials as long as his name. He was a rich landowner, son of an English knight, Commander of the 88th flying squadron in the United States Army during the First World War and a world champion ice skater. With the Smith ranch running at a loss and its foreclosure looming, their daughter's financially desirable marriage may have relieved their worries to some extent. Yet, despite a honeymoon in Europe, study for Katharine in Switzerland, and plans to build a house of some luxury on their return home, after just over two years of marriage Katharine wanted out.

Both families railed against the notion of Robert and Katharine marrying. Katharine's divorce hadn't yet gone through and it was further complicated when Captain Richard ('Major Dick', my father rudely dubbed him) hired a private detective to shadow his rival. Yet the romance continued in whatever place and time the lovers could manage, usually at the house of Katharine's Aunt Hattie.

During one clandestine telephone call, Richard Shipley grabbed the receiver from Katharine and issued Robert with a threat: 'Come onto the Smith ranch at twelve noon tomorrow and I'll meet you with a gun.'

Crazed with love, or wanting to prove to Katharine he had the same fire in his belly as her brothers, my father furnished himself with a weapon and transport. He found his old schoolmaster, who he knew to be in possession of a 45-automatic gun, and borrowed it. His buddy 'Specs' lent him his LaSalle car. And on the click of midday the following day, the armed lover rolled into the Smith drive in a car suited to Al Capone, with huge white-wall tyres and a running board that could have held a number of henchmen.

Heart racing, he listened for a creak on the screen door, for footsteps falling on the porch. Nothing. He honked the horn but Captain Shipley was AWOL. Waiting not a minute more than necessary to win hero status, he drove off, unmolested and honour intact.

But having given up his position on the painting crew to be close to Katharine, he was a jobless hero. The only occupation that drew him away from Fullerton was his singing, travelling to Los Angeles to study on his Zoellner scholarship.

Hardesty Johnson, the famous tenor and Julliard instructor, proved himself to be a brilliant teacher and the catalyst that would turn the amateur into a professional. For the first time my father was taught the importance of diaphragm breathing and, with practice of this technique, he began to truly harness the power of his voice. He started singing classical pieces at prestigious venues, such as the Beverly Hills Hotel.

When the scholarship finished, he continued with lessons, hungry for more instruction. But finally Johnson cut his pupil free by telling him: 'You'll never need another lesson, that's it, you'll sing all your life. Get experience, it's the only teacher you need now.'

Unfortunately, that teacher wasn't advertising in neon.

He auditioned for the popular bandleader and pianist, Gus Arnheim, who played at the Coconut Grove in the Ambassador Hotel in Hollywood. Standing next to Arnheim's piano, looking out over the vast dance floor and dining tables spread out under decorative coconut palms, his nerves didn't get the better of him. He sang extremely well.

But he made one big mistake—a mistake easy to make when you are knocking on the door of the famous. Despite every fibre in his body wanting to lead, he didn't. Instead he followed Arnheim's beat, deferring to him, following his interpretation and not insisting on his own. Although the bandleader liked what he heard, his assessment was: 'Come back . . . after you've got some more experience.' Leaving the young man asking himself: 'Where the hell am I to get more experience if everybody is going to say the same thing?'

Towards the end of 1931, my father's family became deeply concerned about his future. His singing career wasn't taking off and, despite relentless pressure to end the romance with Katharine, the love affair stubbornly endured. So a plan was devised that would put distance between the lovers and deliver a weekly wage in the bargain. His Aunt Bess and her husband had failed with their paint store in Fullerton but now enjoyed success with a similar venture in Honolulu. Bess's husband made his nephew an offer: an apprenticeship in his thriving painting business and the hospitality of their home until he found his feet.

Promising Katharine they would be wed in Hawaii as soon as he could save money to send for her, in early January of 1932 Robert Cutter sailed for Hawaii.

—

My FIRST DESTINATION OUTSIDE Australia in the mid-seventies was Honolulu. On a tight budget, I managed to afford one of the cheaper rooms in the Royal Hawaiian Hotel. I wanted to make a pilgrimage, and soak up the atmosphere of the place in which my father had made his name; to stand on the lawns by the terrace where he had stood for publicity pictures surrounded by his big band, to see where he sang through a megaphone in the tropical terraced gardens under light from hanging lanterns. But although the Royal Hawaiian retained a retro glamour, with its pink stucco façade shaped into a romantic mix of Spanish and Moorish architecture, in crucial ways I was too late. In my father's day the 'Pink Palace', with its four hundred rooms overlooking the ocean and six-hectare garden cooled by trade winds, reigned supreme. Then, only two hotels sat on the beach: the Royal Hawaiian and the Moana.

He lived a life there that was glamorous by night and simple by day. I remember him telling me that in Honolulu he never used an umbrella. He said if it rained while he was walking he'd be dry by the time he arrived at his destination. I imagine him now, moving in dappled light through avenues of trees, the sound of his sandals echoing in quiet streets, and the scent of frangipani, hibiscus, jasmine and honeysuckle floating from gardens built around white stucco walls. By the time I arrived, the crush of buildings and the clamour of tourists had all but obliterated the world my father knew, before Hawaii became the fiftieth US state in 1959.

In the 1930s, not one building on the sandy ribbon of Waikiki curtained the view of the volcanic headland of Diamond Head, the rocky peninsula that crouches like a gigantic lion guarding the entrance to paradise. At the time of my father's arrival, the 'deep strong charm' that had affected a swooning Mark Twain over half a century before was still wholly intact.

My father had walked into the heyday of Honolulu, into a city that had escaped the worst of the Depression. At that time, it was an exclusive and exotic destination that rivalled the French Riviera. The wealthy travelled from California in great style and, after a week of luxury aboard a ship designed to ease them into Eden, these black-tie tourists disembarked from their teak-decked liners, ready to be entertained royally at the Royal Hawaiian.

But shortly after my father's arrival, news came that his beloved grandmother, Blanche Conkey, the woman who had raised him, had died. It was her seventh stroke. Before he departed she had been bedridden. When he had said he was putting off his trip, her unselfish answer was 'No, no, no.' She died on his twenty-fifth birthday just after hearing her 'dear Buster', as she always called him, was with her daughter, Bess, in Honolulu. He always believed she waited until she had learned of his safe arrival.

Just weeks before her death and before his departure, Blanche had gathered the family together for Christmas. Bess travelled over from Hawaii and the table was crowded with extended family. But there was one person missing: her daughter, Louise— my father's mother. Despite several pleading letters from Blanche to her daughter, telling her she was sickly and needed to see her just 'once more . . . before the call comes for me to quit', on the day Louise was absent.

So it was now that his Aunt Bess assumed the role of mother to my father. For six months he roomed with her and it was she who, at one of her musical soirees, orchestrated the meeting that led to the first big break of his singing career.

After hearing my father sing at Bess's, the editor of the *Honolulu Advertiser* arranged for an audition at the newspaper's associate radio station, KGU. He got the job and that first half-year was packed. In jeans and paint-splattered shirt, he'd clamber from the cab of a two-ton delivery truck in his break from 'learning the paint business', and dash up the stairs of the KGU studio to host and sing on a morning show for the

Dairy Farmers Association. Called 'CreamFreezers', it promoted the delights of ice cream through a trio known as Mr Velvet & his Varieties. Within a month, things were going so well he quit his job at the paint factory. Robert Cutter was Mr Velvet, the smooth crooner, while Old Popsicle played guitar and Big Milknickle alternated between piano, clarinet and organ. Mr Velvet was the mainstay of the program, carrying the title of scriptwriter, manager and compere.

He then moved to KGMB. The signal from this radio station would later unwittingly lead the Japanese to Pearl Harbor; but for now, for my father, its signal would only lead to success. In just under six months after his arrival, Robert Cutter was being written up in the press as a tenor with 'a large following of ardent admirers', as a singer who was 'winning many new friends in Hawaii', as 'a young man who sings like a veteran', and as an entertainer 'who will make a big name for himself'. When he wasn't on KGMB airways, he sang about love at weddings and about God in churches. He appeared at college alumni dinners, at YMCA concerts and with dinner dance bands.

In June 1932, he was employed by musician, arranger and orchestra leader Johnny Noble and was singing at the Moana Hotel. Noble thought so much of his tenor that he used Robert Cutter's arrangements and, when he travelled to California, he left my father in charge—not only as the singer in the band but as manager of the radio broadcasting program bookings, salaries and rehearsals. He was averaging a working week of eighty-five hours.

In the few afternoons my father had off, he'd go down to the beach, loll on the pink sand and watch 'The Duke', Halapu Kahanamoku, the Olympian 'human fish', swimming freestyle among the board riders and outriggers. He told me once that the mastery of it inspired him and now I wonder if, for the first time in his life, he felt that he, too, had the potential to go for gold.

To achieve his dream of bringing Katharine to Hawaii, for six months my father put aside all he could of his salary, and every night he wrote to his fiancée, even though he knew he would need to wait at least a month for the fortnightly boat mail to deliver a reply.

At the end of July, Katharine Smith finally arrived. Her husband-to-be was waiting at the wharf, carrying a lei of flowers for her neck and a ring for her finger. Cutter was 'all a flutter' reported the *Honolulu Advertiser,* which ran a large photograph of the photogenic couple in its pages. Within the six short months he had been in the islands, he had turned his life around and was at the start of a successful career. How it must have pleased him to know that Katharine's disapproving parents would be reading this report in their Californian paper: 'Mr. Cutter and his bride-elect have been friends since they were children. They plan to make their home in Honolulu, where he is prominent in musical circles. He is at present a featured radio singer.'

When Katharine's ship sailed from California, there had been a tearful goodbye from her family. As the coastline disappeared, she sat down on deck and wrote a letter that appears to offer not only reassurance to her parents, but to herself:

I don't want you to be blue and miss and worry about me.
You all know I'm going to be awfully happy . . . Bob and
me are going to make a big success of our marriage. If one
makes up their mind to do so it can be beautiful.

Robert had married his best friend's sister. Immediately after
his father's death, in that needy and vulnerable time, he had fallen
for Katharine. Perhaps he was marrying the sense of home the
Smith ranch had given him. A story he told in later years paints
a picture of the young married couple like two kids still crashing
about the orange orchard, simply playing dare. 'One day, just
to see what was possible between breakfast and midnight, we
managed nine beddings.' No surprise then that almost immediately Katharine fell pregnant. It allowed little opportunity for
them to simply be a couple but while time permitted they went
hill climbing, exploring all the loveliness of Oahu together.

In April 1933, their baby girl was born. They both adored
Morneen (soon to be shortened to Miki), and Katharine wrote
to her parents: *'Bob and I can't stop looking at her . . . we're*
a grand happy family.'

But, for Katharine, having a baby so soon became isolat-
ing. Her world shrank in every way. Honolulu seemed small to
her—'No bigger than Orange County'—and, apart from Bess,
she had no family and no one she could call a good friend. Her
husband's busy schedule, often continuing late into the night,
added to her loneliness and homesickness. The baby's progress—
sleeping, crawling, cutting a tooth—became her focus. This,
or baking a cake, or the high price of fresh peaches from the

mainland, were the events on which her life turned and the only subjects that filled the letters she wrote home.

All of the bright hope on the faces of the bride and groom on their wedding day faded rapidly. The marriage would be over in a little more than two years. Whoever was responsible for the break-up isn't clear. In later years, Miki and her father agreed that Katharine's 'unpredictability of attitude' and 'a general intractability about things not seen her way at the time of seeing' had been difficult aspects of her character. Finally, perhaps the problem came down to his simple statement: 'We were pals . . . I outgrew her.'

Although he said he vainly fought for custody of Miki, over the next forty years the only contact his daughter would have with her father were letters, a handful of visits when she was a toddler, and the disembodied sound of him singing on the radio. His own bleak history of being raised without a father was to be repeated. And, just as my father had relied on his grandmother for love and care, Miki, would, in most part, depend on her grandmother Lenore Smith.

By the time Katharine sailed home with the toddler, my father's career was in ascendency. He was everywhere, doing everything. He had risen to the rank of production manager for radio KGMB, a station he was steering to success, soon to take number one billing away from his old station KGU. He was resident soloist at the prominent Christian Science Honolulu Church. He was singer and host six afternoons a week on a radio program called *Chasin' the Blues*. And, rising above the popular, he received excellent critical reviews after giving a solo concert recital at the Honolulu Academy of Arts. But the biggest game changer came in 1934, when he began singing with Harry Owens's Royal Hawaiian Orchestra and performing at the Royal Hawaiian Hotel.

When Harry Owens arrived in the islands to play at the Royal Hawaiian, he was widely known as a fine arranger and composer. When he hired Robert Cutter, he not only got his lead singer but a trusted adviser, who argued forcefully for the virtue of adding steel guitar, gourds and bamboo sticks to the dance band and adapting real Hawaiian songs to their repertoire. Owens assented and immersed himself in Hawaiian music culture, both traditional and contemporary, and split his band into two: the Hawaiian and Haole (European) instrumental sections.

The Hawaiians gave Robert Cutter their seal of approval: 'He *maikai* [good], no spoil Hawaiian words.' My father, an aficionado of the best musicians in town, swiftly introduced the rhythm guitarist Freddie Tavares to Owens, believing he had the talent to master the steel guitar, which he did within a matter of weeks. Today Fender makes a special edition of guitars in Tavares's name. The songs and music Owens composed, the band he led, were in tune with what became his catchphrase: 'All Hawaiian, all the time.' By the 1940s and 1950s, he would become famous for his music throughout the USA, in part due to my father's initial inspiration.

During and after the marriage break-up, my father leaned heavily on his faith in Christian Science. He gave up smoking, gave up drinking, took constant advice from his Christian

Science practitioner and was at his peak mentally and physically. He was put under contract with Owens's Royal Hawaiians and began cutting records. He was the featured singer on international radio broadcasts and his name and face were on the sheet music of Owens's compositions. He sang at the Moana Hotel under the famous banyan tree that still stands today and, by 1935, he was Honolulu's favourite soloist.

That same year, in the town of Hollywood, a restless woman began making plans to spend the summer months in Hawaii. She went by the name of Rubey and her arrival would change his life entirely.

Chapter Six

Gimme eastern trimmin' where women are women
In high silk hose and peek-a-boo clothes
And French perfume that rocks the room
And I'm all yours in buttons and bows.
'Buttons and Bows', 1947, lyrics by Ray Evans

WOMEN. MY FATHER SANG about them, sang to them, had a string of them. And, as I grew up, I believed he knew all there was to know about them, recognised every requirement necessary to achieve the pinnacle of female beauty, from the curve of a nose to the shape of a leg.

When it came to a beauty parade, he was the judge and jury. In my buckled shoes and short white socks, I stood for inspection, feet tight together, hoping my skinny legs might make the Betty Grable grade while he described just where a space should be seen between the curve of an ankle and the rise of a calf. I got good points until he reached my ankles and pronounced them 'a little too thick'. I still feel a sense of deflation as I type his words.

One particular memory when I was around the age of six, confirms his abiding dedication to the subject of women. He was to perform that night at a concert in the city. It must have been an important venue, for he was dressed in a dinner jacket and bow tie, and my mother was making a particular flourish of an extra good luck wave from the balcony of the terrace in which we were then living. She and I, having called down our farewells as the white paling gate clicked behind him, watched as he made his way up the street, waiting for him to turn one last time. But then he stopped abruptly and gazed towards the middle distance.

For a moment we thought he must have forgotten his security blanket, a small notepad containing handwritten lyrics, always tucked into his pocket ready for a speed-read before each song. However, as we followed his line of vision to the opposite side of the street, we saw the object of his attention. The rhythmic tap-tapping of the high heels of a shapely young blonde had stopped him in his tracks and so mesmerised him that he then turned slowly to watch her progress.

Suddenly, as though he'd heard a click of the hypnotist's fingers, he remembered his wife and child standing above and, with a start, looked up guiltily to find my mother in a fit of laughter. A relieved wide grin, a shrug, his hands palms-up in supplication composed his grateful reply. In his former life, he had almost drowned in showgirls and sequins; but even at my young age I knew that no woman, not even one with perfect legs, could seduce my father away from the life he had embraced with 'his girls': from the woman on the balcony stripped of makeup and all her old finery, and from me—the child he hadn't particularly wanted but loved fiercely nevertheless.

However, I learn now, some memories lingered. In the cool of his seventh decade, he still remembered Rubey, still remembered the heat. *'I had never been kissed like that in my life—never . . . before or since.'* This particular recollection, sealed within an airmail letter, would sail thousands of kilometres from my mother's sight.

His confession was written to my half-sister, living in California. Having been denied her father's presence as she grew, by the time Miki had begun having children of her own she was hungry for facts about her father's past, and details of the family history. Decades later, I would become included in these revealing conversations. By father and daughter being so robustly forthright, by being such good correspondents and by safeguarding each other's letters, they became an answer to this biographer's dream.

—

MARY RUBEY COX WAS a blonde you'd find in a Raymond Chandler novel, 'a blonde to make a bishop kick a hole in a stained glass window . . . whatever you needed, wherever it happened to be—she had it.' She had been born and raised virtually off the map in the village of Stoutsville, in the county of Monroe, in the state of Missouri—home to less than two hundred people in a good year. An unschooled girl, Rubey first married at sixteen. Then she stopped counting—both her marriages and her age. Her date of birth would change on most every form she filled in.

Hers was the classic Hollywood story: a country girl arrives in Los Angeles, gets into the silent movies. Her timing is right. She finds work as a chorus girl and supporting actress with stars on the rise, one being Charlie Chaplin. The sidekick in Chaplin's films, Lloyd Bacon, is on the eve of morphing from actor into one of Hollywood's most successful film directors. Bacon becomes one of the talkies' first directors, and one of the highest paid in the business. Rubey becomes his wife: a 'former actress' who creates an off-screen role for herself as a classic Hollywood femme fatale. Powder blue eyes, blonde hair perfectly styled and pinned, a figure curved and, as they would say in the day, 'stacked' and complete with a pair of perfect 'pins'—this was Rubey: a woman who was all glamour and who perfectly represented the Golden Age of Hollywood. She found it easy to lie about her age. In 1930, she declared to the government on the census form that she was thirty-four, when in fact she was a decade older—an eternity in Hollywood.

Striving to keep that fact hidden must have been a midlife crisis of cosmic proportions in a town full of ambitious hopefuls, dressed scantily in silken high-cut shorts, with thighs of such perfection they passed muster when the camera lens leered just inches away. Rubey was all too aware that her husband, as director of *42nd Street* and other confections spun from the imagination of the legendary choreographer Busby Berkeley, was at the epicentre of these whirlpools of tap-dancing flesh.

Bacon had risen to prominence during the 'Pre-Code' period, when censors were looking the other way. Traditional female 'virtues' were out the window. Barbara Stanwyck in *Baby Face* successfully slept her way to success, while Mae West proclaimed her predatory sexuality with an auctioneer's zeal. But, by 1935, stricter censorship laws were working to restore hearth and home. Innocent little Shirley Temple showed her dimples and the girl-next-door, Ginger Rogers, allowed Fred Astaire to lead. Bing Crosby fitted perfectly, with his comfortable crooning cardigans and Father Chuck O'Malley's clerical collar, into the more righteous times to come.

In 1934, with a bonfire of candles missing on her cake, Lloyd Bacon threw his wife a lavish birthday party. He was the dapper host, impeccably dressed, a clotheshorse with a nod towards expensive hats. The hats were his signature and his barometer as a film director. Whenever an actor missed a cue or didn't perform to Bacon's liking, the hat became a missile, flung before his words arrived to berate the offender. The journey from Hollywood to his estate in San Fernando allowed him to don a different hat at his weekender, that of gentleman farmer.

Movie folk at this time were playing at ranchers on the outskirts of make-believe, and the Bacons, known to possess one of the most beautiful converted farmhouses in the valley, led the way. Soon open-air parties became the Hollywood vogue, and the director and his wife showed their friends how to do it, stringing lights through the trees, serving Mexican food and fruits from their orchard on large rustic wooden platters by roaring outdoor fires. Hal Wallis's wife, Louise Fazenda, quipped that they were purchasing the neighbouring ranch to 'raise white mice and grow raspberries'. When Crosby asked who was going to raise Cain, she retorted: 'Oh, we're going to keep that element out.' On the night of Rubey's birthday party, Bing Crosby was the first to leave. He needed the sleep, he said: he had thought it a good idea to build the nursery next to the main bedroom but he hadn't counted on twins. 'They yell in relays,' he explained to his hosts on his departure.

Crosby's wife, Dixie Lee, was coaxed down from a high tree limb in one of the orchard's fig trees, where she had been perched eating the fruit directly from the branches and gossiping on the same branch with the wife of Pat O'Brien. The Crosbys departed leaving Joe E. Brown to his antics in the swimming pool and off the high diving board, replicating the stunts from his newest picture. Claudette Colbert and other stars of Hollywood rambled through the Spanish hacienda and out into the grape arbour, the swimming pool, the badminton court, the stables, the fruit orchard.

That night, dangling not just one carrot but the promise of many more, Bacon gave Rubey a bracelet designed to display jewel-studded objects that celebrated important occasions. Rubey, computing that St Patrick's Day was soon arriving, immediately liked the idea of a shamrock detailed with diamonds: 'It would be just too cute,' gushed a gossip columnist.

Before a year was out, such trinkets would be cast aside. Instead, alimony claims and real-estate deeds would be laid out on a long negotiating table in a divorce case that hit the front pages across the country. Five months before her marriage to this powerful Hollywood director spluttered to its messy halt, in June 1935, Rubey had sailed for Honolulu, where she found a good reason to torment Lloyd Bacon into divorce proceedings.

When she sailed into Honolulu on her white ship, Rubey rivalled Cleopatra—pampered, perfumed and resplendent in her haute couture. She rented one of the finest houses at Kahala in which to hold court. The gossip columnists for the *Honolulu Advertiser*, and the island's florists, were kept busy:

A supper dance honours Mrs Lloyd Bacon . . . fifty friends were invited to enjoy the evening.

Giant gardenias, tall white tapers and ferns decorated tables at the dinner party honouring Mrs Lloyd Bacon at the Royal Hawaiian.

Mrs. Margaret L. Smith entertained at a cocktail tea Thursday afternoon at her Diamond Head home in honor of Mrs Lloyd Bacon . . . Hawaiian music was played . . . pikake leis were presented to the honoured guests.

Exactly when Rubey first met my father is unclear, although records show they sailed from San Francisco to Honolulu on the same Lurline ship that June of 1935. He had spent six weeks away in California, securing his divorce, broadcasting and cutting records.

Rubey couldn't have escaped hearing him sing—on the radio or gramophone, or at the Moana or the Royal Hawaiian Garden Court, where men wore dinner jackets and women chiffons and satins cut in elegant swathes to the floor. White-clothed dining tables floated through the candle-lit gardens, light from torches on the native fishing boats etched the ocean, and a bright line of sea foam highlighted the coral reef.

Nothing could have been more romantic . . . until the music started and my father sang. He stood in front of the orchestra, in a cabana decorated with palms and flowers, and waited for Harry Owens to lift his baton. When his voice rose and carried across the dance floor, the flower-scented air became sweeter still.

Rubey thought so. She adored what she saw and heard, to the extent that she made her first 'pitch', as my father described it, at one of these Royal Hawaiian evenings. When that failed, she contrived to have her powerful Hollywood friends, Harry and Marie Green, coax him back from a dance night at the Waialae Golf Club so she could, they said, 'meet him properly'.

My father was aware that when he told this story it sounded like a 'dime store novel', the kind of thing that he would normally scoff at. Nevertheless, shouldering his embarrassment, he squarely recounted the details in that letter to Miki.

Once back at Rubey's luxurious home, she called him out to the kitchen to help carry in the drinks. As he walked towards her, she stepped up to him, her red lacquered fingers grabbing his head, and she pulled him down towards her to receive what in his words was 'a cataclysmic kiss'.

He was lost, but Rubey knew the way. She drove him back to the Royal Hawaiian staff quarters and insisted on seeing his room. Once inside, she asked after a certain record he might play for her on his gramophone. After a brief search, having found it, he turned around to find Rubey on his bed, naked.

When Rubey sailed home at the end of that week, a photograph of her shows a woman lassoed in leis. She looks like a girl, with a brilliantly red-lipsticked smile that says she feels exactly like that—young again.

My father, relatively unsophisticated, found himself 'in a bind' and in 'a battle of faith'. He saw himself as 'weak, naïve— a lamb to the slaughter' and, his religion still front and centre, offered his resignation as soloist at the Christian Science church. His practitioner dismissed his request.

But Rubey was not to be rejected, not even across an ocean. While he was in the middle of broadcasting his *Chasin' the Blues* program for KGMB in Honolulu, a radiophone call came through for Robert Cutter from the West Coast—a small technical miracle in 1935. At the end of the line was none other than Rubey Bacon, his determined pursuer, for whom distance would soon no longer be a problem.

———

AROUND AND AROUND WE go. In decades to come, my father would first farewell me and then later my sister, Geraldine, as one after another we left Sydney to follow careers in America. When we departed in the 1970s and 1980s, he didn't harbour the same sinking feeling of misgiving for us that he had for himself in that

August of 1935, when the SS *President Hoover* pulled out of Honolulu and set course for the USA.

Rounding Diamond Head, he threw his remaining farewell lei overboard. As he watched the flowers bob and float and then be dragged down by the wake, doubt and homesickness overwhelmed him. He had left the city that had nurtured his career, fans that hero-worshipped him and, most drastically, he had cut ties permanently with his mentor, Harry Owens, a man in whose ability he had no doubt. 'Impetuous' is how he suddenly saw himself.

His ship had sailed weeks before when, purely out of impatience, he had asked Harry Owens to tear up his contract. Owens had for some time been negotiating a mainland engagement for his lead singer and his band, the Royal Hawaiians. But the deals kept falling through. My father, on his trip to California that June, had met the manager of the renowned St Francis Hotel in San Francisco and auditioned. When, after returning to Honolulu, he received a call that offered him a three-month renewable contract to sing at the opening of the now fabled Mural Room, and to broadcast over the airways from its vast decorative dinner and dance hall, my father decided he couldn't wait for Owens and asked to be set free. The bandleader agreed to tear up the management agreement with one proviso: 'Don't ask to come back if you aren't satisfied.'

There was hype at his announcement; the press called it the 'big break' for the 'golden-voiced' crooner. But it wasn't the promise of popular fame that made my father's heart beat faster. It wasn't the quickened rhythm of 'hot' music, as they called it, but the tempo that swayed serious audiences in the Honolulu Academy of Arts. Over the two years of his singing career in Honolulu, he had given two recitals singing classical songs in those hallowed halls, to both large audiences and critical, applause. He was a crooner who wanted to be a 'legit' (his word) tenor—tails rather than tux, orchestra rather than band. When he sang Brahms rather than Berlin, or Schubert, Schumann and Strauss rather than Porter, Kern and Carmichael, critics noted his 'purity' and 'power'. One predicted: 'With further development under proper tutelage [Cutter] could achieve much greater eminence . . .' They were pleased to note that he had stopped, for a brief moment, 'entertaining Joe Public'. But for the foreseeable future it was Joe Public who paid my father's bills. He hoped that exposure in San Francisco might hasten his dream of becoming a classical singer.

And so he exchanged a tropical beach for a fog-cooled city, one hotel room for another (his new contract included accommodation in the staff quarters at the St Francis). For a slightly lesser salary (sixty dollars a week) he followed the baton of Hal Grayson rather than Harry Owens. The glamour became formalised. As the dancers turned in tighter circles in the bigger city, the only scent drifting through the air was imported perfume. In his first month at the St Francis, he shared the news columns with Bing Crosby and Gary Cooper and, in the words of one critic, he was 'kicking ether dust in the faces of all other local dance band singers'.

At the much heralded, very grand opening night, he knew he could expect to see Rubey in one of the best seats closest to the stage. Some time back she had planted a story in the Honolulu press that she would be there, travelling up from her Hollywood home to cheer on the singer, whose voice she 'loved'. And there she was, shimmering in jewels and finery, applauding every move he made. She stayed with him that night, and for the week following, and he was 'gone'.

So, too, was Rubey's marriage. In three months, she would be divorced. Her husband, if he had any doubt about their state of marital disharmony before she travelled north to San Francisco, would have had none upon her return.

In between his movie making, Bacon had taken to hiding out in a barn on his Hollywood ranch. Here he accommodated his favourite pastime, playing trains. The miniature railway—a web of main lines, branch lines, junctions, terminals and rolling stock—dominated the entire building. The model was of such magnitude that Bacon gave it a name: the California-Southwest Lines. Overseeing this complex, Bacon was in charge of all comings and goings, keeping all running smoothly and on track. When he could no longer deny this was the only place in his home where he had control, and realised that Rubey (unlike Garbo, who was playing the role of Anna Karenina in the cinema at the time) had no intention of throwing herself under any train, he sued for divorce on the grounds of mental cruelty.

Meanwhile Robert Cutter was in discussion with the Fleishackers, a family of such wealth they took up a whole floor of the St Francis hotel as a town residence. They had attended the last concert at the Honolulu Academy of Arts and liked what they heard. Now they had it in mind to support the hotel's resident singer by sending him to Europe to study. He was at a critical point in his career—the classical stage beckoned.

That dream ended when two uniformed deputy sheriffs strode purposefully under the palm trees and chandeliers and through the glamour of the Los Angeles Palomar Ballroom. While my father sang they stormed onto the stage and into the spotlight. Then, to the amazement of the audience, they clicked handcuffs on the singer in the middle of his song. As they marched him out through the thousand-strong astonished onlookers it was a sight so bizarre that some believed it must be part of the show. But no. In these last days of November 1935, it was just the beginning of a scandalous circus involving Lloyd Bacon and Rubey, my father and other players, that would mean litigation and court hearings stretching across the next four years.

At Bacon's instigation, the warrant for Robert Cutter cited contempt of court and detailed his failure to appear at 6331 Hollywood Boulevard for a deposition to be used on Bacon's behalf at the forthcoming divorce trial. Newspaper front pages headlined, 'Crooner Arrested in Film Love Case', and carried his photograph under the banner, 'Accused'. This sat above a larger picture of Rubey and Lloyd Bacon from a happier time, both looking resplendent in nautical gear, posing for the camera aboard their yacht.

Already the papers had been full of the divorce, with Rubey complaining that temporary alimony of $2225 a month was necessary to pay for her 'immediate needs'. Considering the country was in the grip of the Depression and that the highest paid Californian labourer, if he was lucky enough to be in work, toiled to take home $250 a month, it's not difficult to see why the judge believed one line item—$200 a month for beauty treatments and cosmetics—to be excessive.

However, he allowed that she needed to pay the salary of two servants. When she was cross-examined on the $750-a-month claim for clothes, she explained her distaste for repetition: 'I just don't wear them and *wear* them.' When Lloyd Bacon revealed he had taken the time to count the number of shoes Rubey possessed, his calculations must have struck a chord of sympathy in the court—with 320 pairs in her closet, his wife had still gone walking.

But the ex-actress wept on the stand, citing years of unhappiness, indifference and threats of violence as the cause of the split. 'Many times my husband came home from work, changed his clothes and then went out again without telling me of his plans,' she testified. 'If I asked him questions all he said was, "Don't bother me." On the day we separated, he telephoned me and told me I had better get out of the house by midnight or he would break every bone in my body.'

Bacon countered this, claiming violence by 'nagging'. Rubey's tongue-lashings, he told the ironically named Judge Valentine, had been so vicious the 'stress had affected his work'—and with his work earning him $2500 a week, he couldn't afford it. Besides, she was 'rude to his guests'.

It was easy to become the butt of jokes in the small town of 1930s Hollywood. In his vaudeville days, Bacon had played the fall guy alongside Chaplin in the early silent films. Now he found his life playing out like the torn-from-the-headlines movies he directed at breakneck speed for Warner Brothers. Rubey, who in her silent film roles was the damsel in distress, was now playing the gold-digger, the cheat. And he, after fifteen years of marriage, was cast as the sap. So the director cried, 'Cut!' It was all over just before Christmas 1935.

While newspapers spoon-fed this Hollywood trifle to Depression-poor readers struggling to put bread on the table, my father was making headlines of his own. The Palomar was a dream gig: my father and the band following hard on the heels of Benny Goodman, introducing the swing era under that very roof just months before.

While performing at the Palomar with Grayson, Robert Cutter was written up as a 'brilliant young tenor' and a *'risen young star'*, but his arrest not only halted the accolades, it ended the scholarship to Europe from the Fleishackers. When the divorce and my father's part in it were made public, that offer was withdrawn.

He had suffered the indignity of being hauled from the glittering Palomar dance hall, locked in a police van and taken off to the slammer, where he was held on $1000 bail. Correctly deducing that this spectacle had been contrived by a jealous husband to kill his rival's career, he filed for damages of $50,000 on the grounds that the charges had been improperly drawn. But at Rubey's request he dropped the case, despite being a shoo-in to win it. It was an inducement to Bacon to settle the divorce.

Some months later, in the vast splendour of the Los Angeles Biltmore Bowl, at the eighth Academy Awards ceremony,

Robert Cutter stepped up to the microphone and prepared to sing. Then, for one sprung-lock of a second, he froze. He had spotted his tormentor, Bacon, just six metres away from the stage. Memories of the Palomar fiasco flashed before him, but he didn't miss a beat. Jimmy Grier's big band swung in behind him as his voice filled the room full of hopeful nominees— among them Bette Davis, Katharine Hepburn and Clark Gable.

Bacon didn't relish his seating plan either. He had endured enough embarrassment over Rubey. Now forced to confront the singer close up, he shifted uneasily in his chair. He was only too aware of how his own tough, irregular features compared to this handsome man, who had the added advantage of being a decade younger.

Bacon knew he'd been rash pushing for the arrest and, when he wasn't feeling jealous rage, he knew the young man up on stage hadn't stood a chance against the seductive, insistent Rubey. Still he had enjoyed returning a little of the public humiliation, until his punishment backfired and Cutter sued for false arrest, hauling the whole messy business back on the front pages.

This night, forced to sit so close to his rival, any sense of empathy evaporated. He was the most commercially successful director in Hollywood and yet he had no nomination, no Oscar coming his way this year. What was the point of having such power in this town and yet being put in the position of a prime chump—listening, while everyone in the industry looked on, to love songs sung by the man who had stolen his wife?

He resolved to have lunch with the leader of the band, his old Masonic mate Jimmy Grier, and then Cutter would be sacked. For a follow-up punch, his pal Pat O'Brien, a contract actor with Warner Brothers, would threaten to beat up the young Lothario, rearrange his perfect set of teeth. This would provide Bacon a little satisfaction.

My father kept his teeth but lost the job. Several weeks after the Academy Awards ceremony, Grier was seen lunching with Bacon. Shortly after, the singer was without a band.

Still, it was a heady time for the lovers. There were great celebrations heralding in 1936 at the Los Angeles Shadowland nightclub. The popular tenor was back performing with his old bandleader Hal Grayson and had been held over due to demand. One critic bubbled that the show was full of 'snappy new numbers' and 'snappy new routines'.

Shortly after, Robert and Rubey married in Mexico. This was rash in a number of ways, primarily because they were both still married to other people. Divorce in California was subject to an interlocutory period of one year (equivalent to a decree nisi) before it became final. My father's divorce was due to be finalised in September 1936, and Rubey's not until December of that year.

It had been just a little over six months since my great-grandfather, John, had acted as attorney for his grandson's divorce from Katharine. And given Rubey was no novice in such proceedings, now marrying for the third time, it is reasonable to assume they both knew what they were doing—flouting the law with a marriage that was far too 'snappy'.

Bacon knew enough to wait until his divorce from Rubey was final before he remarried (a marriage that would last less than three years). My father, on the other hand, was a bigamist living with a bigamist.

Chapter Seven

THEN ALONG CAME A tall sophisticate, Jay Whidden. He was a man as easy in top hat and tails as in his cowboy saddle, and as well known in London's West End as in Hollywood. A veteran composer and bandleader, he needed a tenor and invited my father to replace his featured singer, who had left the band to perform in the popular *Burns and Allen Show*.

This was a great opportunity and my father leapt at the offer to sing in the fabled Miramar Hotel in Santa Monica with its bungalows and fountains in landscaped gardens, home from home for Greta Garbo and Jean Harlow. At the end of that successful summer season of 1936, Whidden arranged for his singer and the band to set off on an extensive tour of the mid and southern states.

It's hard to imagine Rubey taking to the gypsy life. However, she was happy enough to marry my father once again, in January 1937, just after her divorce became final and when they were in Texas, staying at my father's singing venue, the St Anthony Hotel at San Antonio, touted then as the most lavish and modern hotel in the world. Nearby was the Alamo, where a famously futile battle had been waged in the city the previous century— this time it would become the backdrop to a personal war that nobody won.

Perhaps Rubey toured with my father, from state to state and town to town, simply because she loved him. Among Rubey's alimony demands (the servants, the wardrobe, the cosmetics) there had been a fascinating request—costs towards fees for her Christian Science practitioner. What this suggests is that Rubey was serious, to the extent she was willing to attempt to adopt my father's strict beliefs.

Yet, how long did they adhere to the dictums of the church? Not long is a fair bet. For one, the founder, Mary Baker Eddy, strongly advocated celibacy and made it clear to followers that, whenever possible, it was better not to marry. Secondly, there was Eddy's belief that the material world is purely an illusion.

That particular illusion immediately became a reality for my father. The boy who had been denied college because of lack of funds, who had struggled through the Depression, who had forged a career while holding down multiple jobs, found himself living in Hollywood-style luxury courtesy of his wife. He drove the newest car on the road, stayed in the best rooms in the best hotels, enjoyed Rubey's lavish Los Angeles apartment and allowed her to dress him. During his trips to the tailors, every sharp sartorial accessory was his, at a nod of his head.

At home and on stage, he was adored. He would receive requests to sing from stars popping up in his audiences—the likes of Nelson Eddy, Jeanette MacDonald and Gene Raymond. Everyone loved him: the sound of him, the look of him. Dressed in a black shirt and white tie, he had sleek dark hair, blue eyes and a killer smile. Although billed as 'The Ace of Tenors', he was every inch the other name he answered to within the confines of the band—'Sweet Man'. Translated, it meant that he sang the music as it was written, but with great expression.

He was the equivalent of a rock star. He was certainly not the man I remembered, who insisted on clear, concise diction and perfectly grammatical sentences. In one article, a journalist bemoaned that Robert Cutter's 'ordinary conversation needed translating'. Many column inches were devoted to my father's jive talk, the new idiom used by musicians to separate their night from day world—most of which is today accepted vernacular. 'The aim of every band,' my father informed the journalist, is to 'get with it, or in the groove.' When musicians met and played for the fun of it, it was a 'jam session'. They were the 'cats' or 'gates'—singers and swingers. If the band was required to play a lunch session when they'd rather be sleeping, it was a 'bring down'. When I was reading this, and hearing my father's muffled slang through the yellowed newspaper report, I realised that before this man became my father, he was Daddy Cool.

Perhaps all the attention went to his head. Maybe there was role-playing that didn't work: he the child she never had, and she the mother he never had. Whatever the magnetic attraction, Rubey, by giving him every material thing, stepped into that role. And he, allowing himself to be spoiled by her, soon began to behave like a brat. With Christian Science out the window, he drank. With all sense of the worth of money lost, he gambled. If he ever looked at himself squarely, he wouldn't have seen much trace of the purposeful young man with the high ideals that Rubey had fallen in love with. He had become one of Scott Fitzgerald's 'careless people'.

When he drank whiskey, it was like a needle jumping its groove. Something about that fermented grain interfered with his brain waves. Decades later, as he walked through the door of our home, the set of his mouth, acid-etched, would signal he had been drinking whiskey. Unless he was given a wide berth, we were in for a night of argument, sometimes so bitter that he would turn a sliver of truth into the sharpest of cutting implements. The slash and burn of words was always made more brutal by the thrust of his powerful voice. 'Yelling?' he'd query. 'Who's YELLING?' He'd project as if he were in a concert hall.

My mother always stood her ground. She was never cowed. But as I grew older, I became aware her distress was deepened by the knowledge that the staid neighbours couldn't help but hear my father's outbursts. Sensing her humiliation, in my mid-teens I would take up her cause and angrily propel myself into the arguments, which only further fuelled his tirades.

It was on one such night he revealed that, when he had married my mother, he hadn't wanted children—which meant that he hadn't wanted me. His old-fashioned, chauvinistic mindset was another topic on which we'd clash. He saw females as the weaker sex. It showed pleasantly in his opening of doors and walking on the kerbside of the street when escorting a woman, and unpleasantly by believing that putting out the garbage, lawn-mowing and occasionally helping with cleaning up the dishes were the only jobs required of a man about the house. One night, when he proclaimed, 'We give you babies!' my burgeoning feminist views were so challenged that I literally stood toe to toe with him, believing I was pushing him to the point of hitting me. He didn't.

But by the time my sister Geraldine grew into a provoking teenager, he lost his restraint. Once, employing a dual punishment of both pain and shame, he pulled her down the hall by her hair in full view of a visiting friend of hers. In another whiskey-driven rage, unable to curb his fury, he picked up his plate of spaghetti and aimed it directly at her across the table.

———

HE HAD BEEN DRINKING on the night he crashed their car and Rubey broke her collarbone. The accident happened just days after their second wedding. And so with Rubey unable to party, and my father being feted and out late drinking with the musicians, one night a doozy of an argument ensued. He was reckless, both with his driving and his words. Finally Rubey, with a broken collarbone and bruised heart, headed back to Los Angeles and Robert Cutter toured on without his wife.

The band continued successfully towards its big finale, scheduled for the Waldorf Astoria in New York City. However, an ill-considered venue in Denver put paid to those plans. The small dance band, strictly oriented to intimate performances in society rooms, was lost in the huge ballroom. Bad attendances followed, and the booking agent M.C.A. (Music Corporation of America) chose to delay the prestigious Astoria job for a couple of months, sending the band back to Dallas. Whidden, furious, broke the contract and his singer headed to Los Angeles and his disaffected wife.

But Rubey was gone. Sail away—that was her go-to plan when her marriages unhinged. By July, she was in Honolulu looking for adventure, then cruising onto New Zealand and Australia. By August, she was back in Hawaii, wooing a new lover. By November, she had obtained a divorce from Robert Cutter in Chihuahua, Mexico, even though, once again, she knew this wouldn't be legally recognised in the USA. And by December, she had married again in Reno, Nevada.

Three things were familiar about Rubey's fourth 'I do': the groom was far younger than the bride; the marriage was bigamous; and she kept adding names. She was now Mary Rubey Bacon Cutter Reynolds—add on to this list her first and last husbands' surnames and she was well on the way to possessing a name that could claim the entire alphabet.

Her new husband, Douglas Reynolds, was described in the press variously as 'a hotel operator' and 'a successful Honolulu business man'. His photograph shows him sporting a high-crowned felt hat, a pencil-thin black moustache and a wide-lapelled trench coat cinched at the waist, looking far more like a Damon Runyon character leaning across a downtown bar than one seated at a boardroom table. In fact, his true occupation did involve leaning across a bar. He was acting manager of a Waikiki beach club for his half-brother who, when interviewed, was reported to say that if Douglas never returned he would be happy.

In a matter of months, Rubey's marriage to Reynolds would be annulled, but not before my father had made headlines again by confronting the couple as they walked into their Hollywood hotel lobby early one morning in late December 1937. It was a short and unsweet exchange that started with punches and ended with the police being called, and both men hauled to night court.

The reports differ as to who said what, who received the black eye and who issued the cut lip. The hotel clerk said he 'wasn't sure'. According to the newspapers, Reynolds said: 'You know you've hurt me.' 'So what,' replied Cutter—and threw the first punch.

In court, my father maintained that it was Reynolds who, when asked if he had anything to say, answered with a hard right. Breaking the peace even further Rubey screeched expletives from the sidelines. However, two court cases later and there would be no more jousting for Rubey. Her tangled brace of husbands would be reduced to none.

My father had begun by missing her badly. While on his continuing tour with Whidden, from his hotel room in Shreveport, Louisiana, he penned a song for Rubey—its refrain:

Into each lonely hour you seem to come and go
The happiness you bring you'll never, never know
For tho you left me, you left me too, so many memories
  of you.

The realisation that Rubey had permanently walked out had been slow. It shows in letters written to her between May and September, later quoted in the divorce case.

In May they were together briefly, and he was all business in her presence, writing out an IOU for a hundred dollars he had borrowed and putting a seven per cent interest rate on his repayment. Apart from paying off a bad gambling debt, he needed funds to send to his ailing grandfather back in Fullerton.

Over the next four months, he seems conflicted, punch drunk with the notion of how life had been with Rubey and how it might be without her. The overriding subject is money, and he plays both prosecutor and defence. On one hand, he insists her money has been his downfall and, on the other, to help him break into the movies, he enlists Rubey's help. '*Certainly I've made it plain enough that I don't want a penny of what has become a curse, YOUR MONEY! . . . We could struggle on what I make.*' And '*Money was no false God to me before I met you.*' And '*I have a big program of education and preparation mapped out for the next three months if you can bring yourself to invest any money in me.*'

If marriages are unknowable from without, theirs was truly opaque. Rubey appears also to be in a state of high emotional flux. Sometime between May and before she marries Reynolds in November 1937, she writes to my father:

My precious darling . . . last night together will always be a beautiful memory. It was so heavenly dancing with you and you were very sweet and lovable and attentive . . .

I've regretted a million times we had had those stormy sessions ... I'll always love you, darling, with all my heart and there never has been anyone but you ... You're the sweetest and most precious person in all the world. Your Rubey.

By June 1938, when the divorce case eventually came before the Superior Court, all love was lost. Both parties submitted their partner's private correspondence before the judge and created a perfect re-run of the Bacon divorce: Rubey suddenly issuing battery charges against my father, and he accusing her of cruelty. Money was on the table: Rubey claimed it all, while my father asked for $22,000 in consideration of the $50,000 due to him when he dropped the false arrest suit against Bacon.

Even by Hollywood standards the story was worthy of headlines: the big-time movie director, the ex-actress, the nightclub singer, his false arrest, the bigamous marriages, the hotel brawl, the string of divorces. Once again, in newspapers around the country, my father was drowning in notoriety.

Cutter Divorce Battle Opens
Discord with Three Husbands Related in Court
Orchestra Singer Denies Wife's Cruelty Charge
Crooner Honoluluan Battle Over Bigamy
Wife Cheers Husband's Rival in Hotel Fight
Freed Again: Wedded to Three Different Men in Two and
    One-Half Years

Perhaps Rubey's personality held sway with the judge; maybe her money purchased better lawyers; perhaps it was lack of evidence. But, in June 1938, Robert Cutter was tossed from the eye of the hurricane that was Rubey, empty hearted and empty handed.

My father further fuelled the bad press by pursuing Reynolds in court. Immediately after the hotel lobby encounter, he took out a suit for alienation of affection. The press called the $60,000 in damages he was seeking 'Heart Balm' for the lost love of Rubey. Despite this embarrassment, despite Reynolds gaining an annulment, he still didn't drop the case, allowing it to stand scheduled for August 1938.

I'm not sure it was simply revenge that drove him on. In my memory, he was always a pit bull with an argument. He'd take certain facts, crunch them hard and, no matter how much reasonable enticement was offered to drop it, he'd rarely let go.

He was now thirty-one years old. He knew that if he had stayed with Harry Owens he would be reaping great rewards. Just after he quit Owens, Robert Cutter's recording of 'Hawaiian Paradise' outsold the covers of Bing Crosby and Guy Lombardo. The Hawaiian music that my father urged the bandleader to adopt was now sweeping the American mainland and making Owens very rich and very famous, with Crosby now stepping into my father's place in the recording booth.

Instead, my father's belief system was shattered and his reputation badly beaten. Pretty much undone, he must have looked back on the slow unravelling, back to the time before the drinking and gambling, before he started losing himself in the excesses that Rubey's lifestyle made possible. He had, as the chaos of the divorce case escalated, sent a telegram to her that was more prophetic than he could have imagined. It read: 'Rubey, Rubey, Rubey. What have you done to me?'

I am sure he would have been grateful that his grandfather had not lived to witness the circus of the court hearings. John Conkey died in August of the previous year, before he could open a newspaper and read of the new mess his grandson had fallen into. John was buried next to Blanche—loving stalwarts, once again side by side, just as they had travelled throughout their lives.

In the early 1960s, my sister Geraldine, aged about seven, was helping our father rummage through a cupboard where he kept his tools. There she came upon a photograph of a curvaceous blonde in a strapless, red-sequinned evening dress. It was a revelation to her: how, she wondered, could that dress be held up without any straps? She asked my father the name of this shapely person. 'That,' he replied, after gazing for some time, 'is Rubey.' She recalls a sigh and then him tucking the snapshot into his pocket. It was never seen again.

By the time my sister was looking at that picture, Rubey was dead. Her life had continued to be played out in the press, on and on in a messy spiral. She made the front pages in 1939, suing her attorneys over her property settlement agreement in the Bacon divorce. The previous year she had been arrested for drunk driving in Beverly Hills, careering down the wrong side of Fairfax Avenue and forcing a State Highway patrolman off the road. While sailing back from one of her many trips to

Honolulu, she'd created a witch-hunt when she declared that $15,000 worth of jewels had been stolen. When asked to open her trunk for the authorities, she dropped the charges, claiming she had lost the key.

A few years before she died, Rubey agreed to marry 'on the spur of the moment' the owner of the restaurant in which she was dining. Early the next morning, they headed off in a chartered plane to Las Vegas. The ceremony in the Wedding Chapel was brief and the return to LA immediate. She died, just shy of sixty, in 1947. The birth date on the death certificate would have been the first time most had set eyes on her real age.

My father never mentioned Rubey's name to me. To Miki he wrote one word to sum up the time he and Rubey spent together: *'incredible'*. Then he added, *'don't expect details here'*. This is a telling dismissal from a man who, in his other correspondence with his first-born daughter, hadn't hesitated to hold back on the minutiae of his seduction by Rubey. I have no doubt that he, a man usually unafraid to admit the truth, had no wish to revive the memory of a time in which he had lost his way.

———

MY SISTER GERALDINE AND I grew up surrounded by a confusion of surnames. Our adopted Dutch grandfather, whom we loved, changed his name from Bosch to van Boss, while our biological English grandfather, whom we never knew and never loved, was called Wallbank. Our maternal American great-grandfather's family had been known as MacConkey, but that got shortened to Conkey. Our paternal name of Cutter—an English name that began long before the mid-1660s, when our forebears became American colonists—that name, the one that had remained intact for centuries, we lost in 1938.

That year my father gazed dejectedly out of a Los Angeles window and heard the truth spoken by a Hollywood agent. It was a truth that had been obvious to him for some months, as fewer and fewer jobs came his way due to the scandal of the divorce. 'Bob,' said the Hollywood agent, 'you can't get arrested in this town.' Perhaps my father recalled the words of W.C. Fields: 'It ain't what they call you, it's what you answer to.' And perhaps, on cue, the clouds parted and a shaft of light hit the façade of the men's clothing store in the street below. Because then, when the agent's next statement came: 'You've got to change your name.' My father knew exactly what that new name would be: it seemed tailor-made, a perfect fit. It came courtesy of the master American haberdashery—Brooks Brothers.

And so the name Robert Cutter disappeared from the gossip columns, and Lawrence Brooks made plans. He intended to pursue an ambition he'd nurtured since Honolulu—to travel to New York and explore the world of music there.

However, before he could head to the East Coast, Jay Whidden, who had stuck by him and employed him as lead singer in a Los Angeles radio program known as the *Court of Musical Jesters*, suggested he take a longer route to reach his destination. Jimmy Campbell—the English songwriter and publisher, impresario, playboy and spendthrift—had proposed an extensive tour of the Antipodes a year before, while Whidden and my father had been touring in Texas. He now made good on that offer. Campbell's ultimate ambition was to create a talent agency in Australia, similar to the M.C.A., booking touring bands and named acts.

Whidden agreed, having previously toured Australia with success and earned the title of 'society' bandleader. However, he insisted that my father, by whatever name he was going by, join him. The plan was to tour Australia and New Zealand for six months to a year and then to travel to London, where Whidden was popular and so well connected he sported cufflinks given to him personally by the Prince of Wales.

A footnote of interest for jazz enthusiasts is that an old friend of my father's, a piano player by the name of Stan Kenton, had been invited to join the group. Cutter and Kenton (as second pianist) had shared a stage at the St Francis, but at this point Kenton couldn't get a job either arranging or 'bashing a piano', as my father put it. Although Kenton was keen to accept the offer, with only a week's notice, the man destined to become a legend missed this particular boat.

On 6 August 1938, the case of Robert Cutter against Douglas Reynolds was marked off the calendar. Cutter's lawyers failed to appear to prosecute. The bitter contest was over—my father had turned his back on it and departed the country five days before. As his ship passed under the newly built Golden Gate Bridge, heading for Australia, there was no sense of regret, none of the doubt that had overwhelmed him when leaving Honolulu. He felt anticipation, experienced a thrill, believing he was 'on his way' again.

Chapter Eight

AS WE CRANED OUR necks to watch my father silhouetted against a burning blue Sydney sky, I saw my mother's anxiety. Labouring on the restoration of our rundown Victorian home, he clambered across the pitched corrugated-iron roof like a high-wire artist, juggling tools and painting equipment, two storeys from the ground. Unlike my mother, I didn't fear for his safety. At the age of six, I believed he was indestructible. I couldn't imagine him ever suffering the smallest slip.

Unharnessed, no sure footing—surely this is how he felt when he first arrived in Australia. Excitement, the sense of new beginnings, had launched him across the Pacific. But landing in a strange new hemisphere and finding himself in Melbourne with its moody climate, which required a winter coat that particular spring, must have induced a shiver at the unfamiliar. And nothing could have been more different to a Coconut Grove or an avenue of palm trees than the heavy stone seriousness of this thoroughly Victorian city. English was spoken, but it was foreign—the accents, the humour, the idiom. The most unsettling aspect: the knowledge that if he were to take another false step, his career would be all but over.

Perhaps the royal welcome rolled out by the Lord Mayor of Melbourne helped put him a little at ease. In early September 1938, Whidden and Lawrence Brooks were feted guests of the Lord Mayor at an afternoon party given in their honour at the grand Menzies Hotel. The walls of the Long Room were proudly hung with a Union Jack alongside the Stars and Stripes, and the chef had gone to the curious trouble of arranging decorative sculptures created from fried bread. While the weather outside denied any notion of spring, inside daffodils and boronia bloomed on the laden tea tables, and sprays of lily of the valley swayed on the ladies' bodices and suit lapels.

It would be the first of many a welcome from the city of Melbourne. The critics billed Lawrence Brooks as 'the singer from Hollywood' with 'a true tenor's voice', and the audiences loved him. Whidden was touting a new dancing-cheek-to-cheek sound, which was softer and more romantic than 'hot' swing. My father helped sell it by writing the lyrics for the theme song for the show, *Sweet Swing*:

We've had our Ragtime,
Had our Jazz time,
Other crazes too
But those have passed, and now at last,
We offer something new
to you

Sweet Swing—it's the latest thing . . .
Maestro play! Sweet, sweet swing.

Whidden's 'Sweet Man', singing sweet swing, was swiftly promoted to the Tivoli Theatre. He shared the billing with an eccentric line-up that changed with the seasons. There were the comedians: the famous vaudevillian Will Mahoney and Australia's beloved comic Roy 'Mo' Rene; variety acts that included jugglers and dancers; Peg Leg Bates who showed Fred Astaire what could be done with just one leg; a black man named 'Snowball'; and an alliteration of acrobats: Dick, Don and Dinah. In a publicity photo, Lawrence Brooks, the most handsome man on the billing, was photographed centre stage. His white suit gleamed in the middle of the long row of variety stars decked out in black tuxedos, while a mix of satin-draped dancers and sequinned showgirls surrounded the performers like the trimming on a Valentine card.

While the comic headliners changed and vaudeville acts were a movable feast, my father was a permanent fixture. Critics extolled his 'fine voice', predicting he was 'a tenor whose popularity is assured'. Billed as a 'topliner', he performed twice a day and toured for two consecutive seasons. His first tour, after his initial Melbourne season, was to New Zealand with Will Mahoney. Returning to Australia, he shared the stage and a dressing room with actor and entertainer Emile Boreo, who had arrived after taking part in the British film *The Lady Vanishes*. When Boreo wasn't entertaining audiences, he held my father in thrall with stories of his stage experiences with the likes of Sarah Bernhardt and Josephine Baker.

When Whidden unexpectedly returned to the States, he was replaced with another well-seasoned bandleader by the name of Roy Fox and June 1939, Lawrence Brooks was sent from Sydney to Adelaide to join Fox on a tour around Australia. Unbeknown to anyone, for five months my father had been suffering severe pain from what he believed to be cancer of the bowel. He would get through his performances by lying down backstage between acts. Often he would miss the finale to sneak off to the cold comfort of his hotel bed. He told no one.

Long before I had any experience of real pain myself, I could see my father was stoic. I remember once, sitting down beside him on his sick bed when he was suffering from a severe bout of rheumatoid arthritis. Just by moving the sheet, I caused him so much pain he cried out. This was an involuntary reaction. I never once heard him complain about the pain he suffered despite, as he grew older, soldiering on through all kinds of ill health. If he had the flu, he'd spend the day heavy lifting in the garden 'sweating it out', he'd say. I don't know what gave him that strength: just plain courage, stubbornness, or a belief in the self-healing powers of the human body, ingrained from his days as a Christian Scientist.

On the fourth night of his tour with Fox, at the Adelaide Town Hall, he attempted to stand for 'God Save the King' and collapsed. He allowed a fellow artist to help him back to his hotel and call a doctor. The immediate prognosis was a suppurating fistula and less than a month to live; he underwent extensive surgery and required two months hospitalisation.

While he was convalescing, he learned that Fox had decided to continue the tour to mainly remote country towns. It proved a flop. The distances were huge, the climate changeable. Members of the troop fell ill with the flu, rain turned into floods and the travelling show was literally and metaphorically stuck in the mud. The old adage, that a USA cross-country tour conquers all but the bravest of bands was one Fox should have recalled, before pitting himself against the Australian outback.

With this failure, Jimmy Campbell ditched all hope of becoming Australia's greatest theatrical booking agent and headed for the port of Perth. As Lawrence Brooks, the man billed by Campbell as one of his 'famous vocalists', lay ill in that Adelaide hospital, Campbell boarded a ship for England, taking with him a twenty-two-year-old female singer from the band, promising her a movie contract.

When my father eventually wired for a significant amount of back pay owed, he was told that Campbell had absconded with everyone's money, including my father's. It was a trouper's nightmare. My father was stranded: his contract void, his fees unpaid, his health frail and some 11,000 kilometres from home. One of Campbell's famous compositions, 'Show Me the Way to Go Home', would have carried a bitterly ironic ring.

Fox remained in the country, scrambling his way out, playing lesser and lesser venues until his departure in September. Lawrence Brooks didn't need to scramble. His reputation was such that by the time he was fully recovered he was hired by the best bandleader in Australia, Jim Davidson, and was singing with his ABC Dance Band. My father, always resilient and pragmatic, took the view that the betrayal by his manager was simply a detour on the circuitous road he was taking to New York City.

He headed to Sydney to live in Kings Cross. In 1939, the area was an international settlement, home to those seeking refuge from European fascism and a haven for bohemians—a self-contained cosmopolitan island on the crest of an inner city hill. He lived in the heart of it all in a flat at the stylish Normandy building, amid the restaurants and clubs and the rainbow of neon signs, with fellow musicians and others who lived off the grid: writers, actors, dancers, gamblers, painters, poets, prostitutes and pimps. Here Lawrence found the city he needed. He drank long and late at the local clubs operating on the sly grog circuit—the Fifty-Fifty, the 400 and the Palms. And he delayed his travel plans.

Working with Jim Davidson and his orchestra—broadcasting on the ABC, touring, recording and performing on various stages including the Capitol in Melbourne and the State Theatre in Sydney—brought a professional satisfaction he had not experienced before. In 1940, a Sydney critic declared that the orchestra delivered 'well-rehearsed rhythms, hot and sweet', adding, 'the band must bow musically to Lawrence Brooks'.

However, Brooks bowed to Davidson. He believed no other bandleader had developed the versatility of the orchestra more, and that with Davidson he was doing 'the most interesting work of all'. He credited Davidson with the fact that he was using more of his voice than ever before, eventually adding four notes: a top note and three lower notes, which allowed him two octaves of range.

The friendships he made with the boys in Davidson's band must have felt a little like being back at the Smith ranch with Stanley and his brothers, and he soon felt at home in Sydney. The beaches lacing the suburbs, streets sprouting palm trees, the temperate climate were all reminiscent of Los Angeles. Not the LA that he had left, which by then was altering beyond recognition, but the city of his youth—before its scale and balance changed with the influx of 'Okies' (migrants from the Dust Bowl) before buildings replaced the orange groves, and before the cars and complicated road systems began to dominate.

Sydney was still a small and gracious city, built on human scale, full of sky and light, and easy to negotiate. He leaned into the Australian way of communication, too. He appreciated the straight-from-the-shoulder, 'fair dinkum' approach, for that was his own modus operandi. He applauded the self-deprecation, the understatement and the irony that came hand-in-hand with the abrasiveness of 'Who are you anyhow?' He appreciated the 'no beg pardons' when it came to expressing honest opinions, and that those opinions, even if diametrically opposed, came laced with tolerance and sociability. He revelled in the rough camaraderie and fitted in by shortening his name—Lawrence to 'Lawrie'—and made friends. Among them he counted violinist and comedian Dick Bentley and Jackie Carpenter, a composer and musician in the band.

One of my father's drinking buddies was bad-boy actor Peter Finch. 'Finchie', who worked for the ABC, lived down the road from Lawrie, but slept wherever he could. Often encouraged by the clientele at the local bars with the offer of free drinks, Finchie would give impromptu performances. He could quiet the most rambunctious of bar rooms with his recitations of poetry—from Byron to 'The Song of Solomon'. His sex life, with the odd prostitute added in, was as catholic as his poetry—the passing parade interrupted here and there by brief notions of matrimony.

One such entanglement was cut off at the pass by a group of Finchie's friends, my father included, who sought to save him from yet another disastrous engagement. They kept him busy at the bar until the clock indicated that the hopeful fiancée-in-waiting and her high society family and friends, who were gathered at the Hotel Australia for the lavish reception, would have all packed up and gone home.

———

These skirmishes paled into insignificance when the announcement of war shrouded the nation. In September 1939, Prime Minister Menzies promised nothing but 'bitter months' to come as Australia entered the Second World War. As my father ordered another round for Peter Finch that night, he couldn't have imagined that at a certain point in the hard years to come he would find himself sharing an army tent with his friend, and suffering at close quarters from the infamous odour of the great actor's socks.

My father wrote that war was 'man's most futile expression, insensate in the fullest sense of the word'. But in June 1941, with Jim Davidson and four musicians, he walked through the convict-built sandstone arch of the Victoria Barracks in Paddington, Sydney, and joined the Second Australian Imperial Force.

He believed Hitler to be 'Hell incarnate' and had grown impatient waiting for his own country to take a stand against him.

While the Entertainment Unit was being formed, my father continued to broadcast and record with Davidson. The 78-rpm records he cut for Regal Zonophone demonstrate that he had a voice for every role, from the romantic to the propagandist. When he sings a ballad like 'Over the Rainbow', his notes cradle and soar, perfectly conjuring a dreamland where bluebirds fly. On the other hand, with a vigour and command worthy of any parade-ground sergeant, his strong, disciplined voice makes a rousing call to arms in the recording, 'Fall In, Brother', insisting: 'Come on, you son of a gun, you'll feel fine as you swing into line.' In 'Who Will Put the I in the AIF', he insists on a change of wardrobe, one where civvies are exchanged for a uniform proudly pinned with the 'Rising Sun'—the army's general service badge. He, an American, makes bold to declare: 'The glorious name of Anzac can never be let down.'

His war years began in the Middle East. During the span of one year the first Entertainment Unit, the 'No. 1 Concert Party', would entertain and boost the morale of over 80,000 Australian troops, as well as men and women of the Allied Forces—British, New Zealand, Greek, Polish, South African, Yugoslav, Czech, Cypriot and Free French Forces.

Corporal Brooks answered to Captain Jim Davidson, and Davidson answered to Lieutenant Colonel Jim Gerald, a veteran of the First World War and vaudeville. Only the best entertainers and musicians would do for Gerald. The army paid for £170,000 worth of theatrical props and equipment, and hired the highest calibre of backstage talent—among them costume designers, seamstresses and electricians. As they were required to be soldiers first and performers second, rehearsals came on the back of two months of full army training.

Then the unit—together with hundreds of crates packed with greasepaint and rifles, ballet dresses and steel helmets and all manner of objects necessary for both theatres of war—were loaded onto the RMS *Queen Elizabeth*. After a rendezvous at sea with the RMS *Queen Mary*, the two mighty ships, escorted by the HMS *Cornwall*, ploughed northwards carrying thousands of badly needed reinforcements.

They landed at Port Tewfik (now called Suez Port) and then rattled across the Sinai in an ancient train, desert sand swirling about the carriages due to the windows being knocked out as a safety measure in the event of a bombing. The railway line didn't simply connect Suez to the Sinai Peninsula and Palestine: it looped back in time to the diggers of the 1st AIF, who had laid the steel tracks to carry troops and supplies in the First World War. Those soldiers would have wept to know that their war wasn't going to be the war to end all wars, and that within twenty-five years the very same tracks would be carrying their own sons to battle.

Headquarters for the unit were established in the former Police Headquarters in Tel Aviv, and for two months they scoured for talent in Syria, Egypt and Palestine, arranged for auditions, co-opted both army and civilian talent, and rehearsed the show. The curtain went up on my father, together with the eighteen-piece orchestra, jugglers, female impersonators, comedians, acrobats and chorus girls, just before Christmas 1941 at the Majestic Theatre in Beit Jirja, 15 kilometres from Gaza.

It was a grand gala opening of the *All In Fun* show. They played to a packed house that included the Commander in Chief of Australian Military Forces, General Blamey, and opened to what would become a theme song, a composition by Corporal Lawrie Brooks, named after the title of the show. From the first act, it was obvious that the effort put into rehearsals had paid off. The pace was fast, the performances polished. It was a spectacular success. Most believed they had not seen a revue back in Australia to equal it. The head of British Army Entertainment allowed it was 'the best show in the Middle East'. While the orchestra was deemed superb, perhaps it was 'Les Girls' who earned the deepest bow. The female impersonators were so successful that they generated a queue of Aussie, Czech and Polish soldiers, waiting for the beautiful dancers after the show. When they exited, the 'stage-door Johnnies' didn't register a blink: the masters of disguise quietly filed past them, unrecognisable in their army uniforms.

On Christmas Day 1941, my father was photographed with his unit—not centre stage this time, just another face in a sea of khaki serge. Despite being the unit made up of the very best of Australia's talent, no name sat at the top of the bill in this theatrical company. On the programs printed in the last year of my father's four-year service, when the unit toured Australian military camps, he was billed as the 'Song Smith'. He was fine with that. He had gladly forsaken his career plans, cast aside any thought of self-promotion, fitted in with the group, become one of the boys. He had journeyed a long way in a short number of years. The glamour boy, 'Sweet Man', had given up his position as front man to become a member of a band of brothers.

How far away his old life must have seemed that December in Palestine when news of the bombing of Pearl Harbor came through. How strange for him to learn it was his old radio station's signal that had led the Japanese to their target. He could not have dreamed of such a thing just five years before, much less imagined that he would be a soldier in an Australian army unit, his voice carried out from Mount Zion across an occupied Europe by the British Forces Broadcasting Service.

They played all the camps in Palestine and then toured with the British 9th Army, entertaining Allied troops throughout Lebanon and Syria. In March, they performed in the grand, French-built Beirut Opera House. The audience, glittering with medals pinned on international dignitaries and high-ranking officers, was of such variety the band played five national anthems.

With the opening notes of 'Jeanie with the Light Brown Hair', Corporal Brooks stilled the vast space. His voice rose to the heights of the gilded roof and pierced the silence in the catacombs below as he conjured love, lost or waiting, in another place and time. Then, to rouse the audience from their reveries, he followed with 'It's A Great Day for The Irish'.

As he hit the last exclamatory note, the theatre shattered with applause. Those present later recalled that the gloved hands clapping in the VIP seats were unable to compete with the stamping feet from the fourth-tier gallery, where desert-tanned Aussies whistled and bellowed, 'Good on yer, mate!' It was a night he would never forget. The show was a huge hit, the *Eastern Times* reporting: 'A revue by professionals is a very rare thing to see in Beirut, especially one of such a varied quality of talent.'

A second tour of Lebanon and Syria followed. During that time they played at the American University in Beirut and in a monastery to black-robed Franciscan monks. Then, when the 9th Division began moving to join the British 8th Division, the No. 1 Concert Party fell in with the long caravan of hundreds of troop-laden trucks moving west. At one point, their full army training was put to use when the unit occupied and defended a bridge point.

Performances were mostly impromptu, given in a wadi among the sand dunes or by the road, up to five or more times a day, to small groups of men so as not to attract the enemy— and never at night: no lights allowed. Often there was no time for scenery, and no time for a stage ... nothing but a couple of floorboards and a truck to act as backdrop and windbreak from the stinging sand. Sometimes the show was interrupted with strafing from German planes as they followed the troops towards the first historic battle of El Alamein. When fighting began the unit was ordered east to await return to Australia, now seriously under threat from the Japanese.

In just a year, my father had pitched tents and helped to construct and deconstruct the huge portable stage over and over again. He had peeled tons of potatoes, driven trucks, and alternated between military squad drills and full dress rehearsals. He had also heard the call to prayer floating across a land that was not yet Israel, listened to lamentations at the Wailing Wall, ridden camels, frozen in the Syrian desert nights, found shade under the cedars of Lebanon, admired the grace of Arab women balancing pitchers on veiled heads, walked amid ancient olive groves, swum in the warm Mediterranean and trekked to the snow-dusted hills that cradled the crumbling ancient city of Jerusalem.

And he had lost a friend. My mother told me this. He never spoke of it and I, running my heedless ways, never bothered to ask where or whether by enemy fire or accident. I now know that a number of men from the unit were lost in skirmishes (although I haven't been able to learn the circumstances) just before El Alamein.

When they finally sailed for home it was on a tramp freighter, MS *Troja*. It was six weeks of high contrast to the outward-bound journey on the RMS *Queen Elizabeth*. The first twenty or so days, the steel deck and rails were too hot to touch. During the second half of the journey home they froze as the ship sailed far south, skirting the Antarctic to avoid enemy fire from Japanese and German raiders. If being on deck was difficult, below deck was impossible. Men hoping for sleep slung their hammocks over the mess tables, while those suffering from the choppy seas were sick on the tables below them. Meals of bully beef, served mostly cold with fat floating on top, did nothing to help the situation. When the salt-water showers were washed overboard in the choppy seas, one water bottle per day was issued for washing and shaving. The toilets, constructed to hang off the side of the boat, were a case of do-or-die in the wild weather.

As the small ship made its way without any form of escort, they were under constant threat. Seven Allied ships had been sunk in the past eighteen months in the same waters in which they sailed. When the smelly old tramp steamer finally docked in Melbourne, the country was in the grip of blackouts and brownouts and rigid controls. Since the beginning of 1942, Japanese submarines had been operating in Australian waters. In February that year, Japanese aircraft attacked Darwin some fifty times, all but destroying that small remote city. A few months later, Sydney Harbour experienced a direct attack from Japanese midget submarines. Australian training camps were full to the brim and ships packed with troops sailed non-stop from Townsville to Port Moresby. After a short leave, the unit was packed onto the SS *Duntroon* and shipped along with them.

The world became mud.

Rain fell and fell and fell. From the dust of the desert they arrived in New Guinea during the wet season—up to ten inches of rain a day. Humidity was high, mosquitoes were rampant, and malaria was commonplace. Costumes quickly became mildewed and the canvas rigging covering the portable stage—enough to cover a fair-sized house—leaked like a colander in the torrential rain.

The entertainers, under Davidson's command, worked in the mud and slept in the mud: in Port Moresby, near the hospitals and camps in the Owen Stanley Ranges, on the edge of the battlegrounds, at Sanananda Point, Buna and Oro Bay; either setting up their meccano set of a stage, complete with curtains, or performing on the fly in jungle clearings, casualty stations and hospital wards. Whatever the circumstances, whether performing to a handful of men or thousands, they never failed to sing, dance and appear to be merry.

The sight of a jeep careering through the jungle with a musician clutching a huge double bass, or female impersonators sitting outside their army tents stitching their frocks, must have been a curious vision. Curiouser and curiouser when one night some of 'Les Girls' picked up their flouncy skirts and alongside musicians, clowns, jugglers, acrobats and a tuxedoed singer, dived into slit trenches when around ninety Japanese bombers flew over to interrupt the show.

In Oro, the Japanese seemed to have politely waited until the end of the performance before their Zero fighter planes came over the bay. Immediately the roles changed and performers became the watchers, looking on as Australian and Allied fighter pilots engaged in a battle they soon won.

Bombers were show-stoppers but mere rain didn't keep the audiences away. In Buna, thousands of rain-sodden, battle-exhausted Australians, plus American GIs and Papua New Guineans (the Aussies' beloved 'Fuzzy Wuzzy Angels'), sat in a semi-circle around a hillside that formed a natural amphi-theatre. Through the blear of relentless rain, they looked down to the bottom of a gully where a small river ran around a stage, and watched a show that opened with the refrain: 'Yes . . . it's all in fun.'

Sergeant 'Wacka' Dawe, a much-loved Australian comedian, generated universal glee despite an audience of mixed nationalities. Simply the look of him—his heavy masculine body, further weighted with a cornucopia of fruit and flowers on his head—managed to induce hails of laughter, even before he began impersonating Carmen Miranda dancing and singing 'Hold Me Tight'. He explained his act in a Pythonesque way: 'It's an imitation of a chap doing an imitation of someone doing an imitation of Carmen Miranda—so any resemblance between myself and Carmen Miranda will be strictly coincidental.'

Coincidental was also the case when 'Wacka', with his enormous girth, donned a sweet little dress and took the role of Cinderella. His opening line, complaining that the tropics had caused him to 'fall away to a shadow', got the first laugh. My father, playing Fairy Quince, had his work cut out promising pumpkins and getting involved in the rough and tumble between the Ugly Sisters, when the Silver Slipper (an army boot) began being used as a rugby ball.

I try to picture my father, wearing a fairy dress, his net skirt swaying as he sashayed around the stage on tiptoe in his army boots, waving a wand. I fail. This is a man I could never have imagined. But this was Lawrie Brooks in New Guinea, fighting the Japanese.

You might think that those left to bury the dead, those left to fight on in nightmarish conditions, would find comedians, acrobats, jugglers, music and song completely incongruous amid the horror. But looking closely into photographs taken at that time, and focusing on the faces of those men as they sat in the rain on that hillside, the miracle is there to see—they were being transported back home, being shown life as it used to be . . . all of them willing it to be like that again some day.

At the same time, there was a great and basic need to find expression for grief and a way to honour the memory of their lost comrades. Dawe would later tell a journalist back home in Sydney: 'One of the most popular songs we put over was "Where's That Old Cobber Of Mine?" written and composed by Corporal Lawrie Brooks.'

My father wrote this song while in the jungles of New Guinea. Embracing the language of his new family, he substituted 'cobber' for the American 'pal'. Today 'cobber' has fallen out of usage but then, when camaraderie was so hard-won, it was used as 'mate' is today. He said the epic Australian advance over the Kokoda Trail inspired the song but, according to my mother, it was personalised by the memory of his friend killed while the unit was stationed in the Middle East.

The sun is in the sky
And the birds still sing
The stars shine at night
It's the same old thing
At least though it seems
When I look around
But deep down inside there's a change I've found
I walk in the sun but I walk alone
The stars are the same we both have known
It all seems wrong to a heart in pain
I ask and I ask, but in vain . . .
Where's that old cobber of mine
Kind of rough still he was fine

He was not much for looks
Not a great hand with books
But his smile and his style, they were grand
Miss that old cobber I do
There'll be no other so true
Through thick and through thin
He was there with a grin
That old cobber of mine
I wonder how he is, that old cobber of mine
Where he is, I wonder is everything just fine
I wonder if he wonders too, somewhere out there beyond
the blue
And long again for days gone by
When we were cobbers
He and I.

These simple lyrics go nowhere near conjuring the love and loss in my father's voice. The sweet high note he hits on the word 'grin' pierces with the pain and courage of those gathered in the jungle, those who determined that laughter and music would be used as a weapon of war—as a lifeline out of a world drowning in blood.

———

IN AUSTRALIA THERE WAS more loss.

Back before he joined the army, in those King Cross days, surrounded by womanisers like Finchie, my father was something of a stand out. A different girl a night didn't interest him.

From a long line of sophisticated hopefuls he chose an ingénue, a young secretary called Gloria Nott. She, with all the slender experience of her twenty-one years, may have appealed because he saw in her a complete reversal of Rubey. I am guessing that at the age of thirty-three, he resolved to give up the ruckus of the late-night bars in exchange for the thing he had always craved as he travelled from country to country, city to city—stability. In July 1940, they married in St John's Church, Darlinghurst, and set up house a short distance away in a flat close to a park and a harbourside bay.

Domesticity didn't last long. A year later, Corporal Brooks, army kit hoisted on his shoulders, boarded the RMS *Queen Elizabeth* and sailed for the Middle East. Sometime between his stints there and in New Guinea, my father's young bride declared that waiting for him was not on her agenda. She explained that she had grown fidgety being left alone, that she had met another man and wanted a divorce.

Throughout my life I never heard him swear. Irritated, he'd mutter 'Nuts'. Angry, he'd exclaim 'Rats!' Red in the face, he'd shout 'HELL'S BELLS!' Resigned, he'd sigh *'maalesh'*— Arabic slang meaning, roughly, 'never mind'. Perhaps, when presented with his runaway bride's news, my father may have used expletives never heard in our home. However, I am sure that, with the defeated weariness of a thrice-married man, *'maalesh'* would have eventually been his word of choice.

Whatever the attraction back then, in later years Gloria Nott didn't warrant more than a shrug of his memory. In the tea chest, I found a photograph of wife number three. She was attractive, but no beauty: a twenty-one-year-old attempting sophistication with a pyramid of a hairdo, a black veil and a lot of lipstick. But he kept this image—perhaps simply for the message she had scrawled to him across the picture—'*I adore you, Gloria*'—to remind himself that adoration is for Heaven and the saints, and nothing to do with the daily work required of love.

The divorce was finalised in August 1944. If he had been a baseballer, he'd have trudged back to the dugout; if a boxer, he'd have thrown in the towel. But my father was a romantic and so he would commit one more time. But this time, for the last time. Like an echo, he would meet a woman of the same name and the same age—one Gloria van Boss.

It was as if the gods proclaimed, '*Maalesh* . . . we didn't mean that Gloria, we meant *this* Gloria.'

Chapter Nine

IN 1941, AS MY FATHER sailed towards the Middle East, crossing yet another ocean, Gloria van Boss stood gazing out of her office window at radio station 2GB in Bligh Street, Sydney. She once wrote how she would watch the jacaranda tree in the garden of the Union Club across the street, as day after day it unfolded its purple-blue flowers. It seemed wrong to her that this joyful thing could still blossom when the family she had found over the last five years had scattered—the comedian, the quizmaster, the news broadcaster, the actor, the singer. Robin Ordell—a golden boy who had arrived straight from school to create his own show, with precocious talent and not yet twenty-one years of age—had joined the RAF to train as a pilot. Charles Cousens, the chief announcer, had enlisted in the army. Jack Davey, entertaining genius, had gone to help establish more Entertainment Units for the 2nd AIF. The sound that represented all this loss, replaying in her head, was the 'horrible, squeaky army boots' of her beloved studio manager, Percy Campbell, beginning his journey to war down the long office corridor with a backward wave.

As the years passed, she'd watched the station grow. Robin Ordell's *Youth Show* and Davey's celebrity blossomed. Then, when war began and newsprint was rationed, Eric Baume, the 2GB newsreader, became the voice that delivered the reports people needed to hear. For those left at home, to take their minds off family and friends on duty overseas, variety shows were good medicine. Despite so much of 2GB talent being depleted by the war, audiences grew larger by the day. Radio beamed into factories as women took the places of their husbands and sons.

My mother, with everyone around her on the move, accepted a job at a sister station, 2CA, in Canberra. They offered her a daily two-hour show to host, combining news and music. She lived in the Hotel Canberra and at the age of twenty-four was, for the first time, free from the restraints of home.

As if on cue, on the train from Sydney to Canberra, she met her first love. They gleamed in each other's reflected light: she remembered he wore the cleanest white shirt she had ever seen and she had a fresh gardenia pinned in her hair. Adrian was his name and he became my mother's fiancé. Bright and witty, he was a psychologist by happenstance, because halfway through his medical degree he'd been unable to find the funds needed to buy the mandatory skeleton to continue with his MD.

The capital city was only a few years older than my mother and almost immediately she felt kinship. The area surrounding her hotel, close to Government House, was, like most of the planned garden city, a budding arboretum. Her home, the hotel, was the hub for war correspondents and political journalists. Among the many to come and go was a friend, Damien Parer, a cameraman who had worked commercially in Sydney, sharing Max Dupain's studio. At the outbreak of war, he began documenting his countrymen in film and still shots in the midst of battle, and earning his reputation as one of the world's greatest war photographers.

She stayed in that job long enough to see the trees of Canberra announce each season just once and then returned to Sydney. Perhaps the distance between Sydney and Canberra was proving too great for the romance, perhaps her mother nagged her about the family being lonely without her. Or perhaps she simply couldn't turn down the highly paid, prestigious position of Publicity Officer for the Colgate-Palmolive Radio Unit, which was located in the same building as 2GB. An ad man called George Patterson, seizing on the new medium, had established a unique and powerful selling platform with the pre-eminent radio unit of the 1930s. Under the Colgate-Palmolive banner, the unit produced all kinds of entertainment, from serials to quiz shows to general entertainment. The job would last but the engagement would not. She ended it when she learned from a third party that Adrian had been involved with another woman.

So when Hitler, his cotton-stuffed effigy emblazoned with a swastika, was thrown off the top of a high office building in Sydney's Martin Place one morning in mid-August 1945, my mother was there. The Japanese surrendered and war in the Pacific had ended. Buses stopped running and police constables gave up directing traffic as streets filled with revellers. The air was thick with joyful noise.

A fighter plane, a Mosquito, took continuous steep turns over the tower of the General Post Office, its loud buzzing competing with the wild cheers, singing, whistles, hooters and gas alarm rattlers. Streamers fell, flags flew, people kissed, hugged, couples danced, British sailors did the hokey pokey and a man, stripping down to the waist, performed a marathon Highland fling. Among the freshly laid flowers at the foot of the Cenotaph, some stood quietly, hats off and heads bowed remembering those who had made victory possible.

Happiness rained down on Martin Place that day. My mother was caught up in the joy but as she stood outside the GPO, taking it all in, Tal, the father of her friend and the bright star from 2GB, Flight Lieutenant Robin Ordell, passed her on the steps. He didn't stop: he didn't see her. His face was wet with tears.

His brilliant son had been killed on one of the last missions of the war. Having told his crew to bail out, Robin Ordell had gone down with his plane. The last thing he had written to my mother from London, where he was getting part-time work with the BBC, was: *'I've had a number of offers for post-war jobs. But it's me for Australia, Poppa and Australian girls. Love and kisses, Rob.'*

Every year that followed, when my mother saw a jacaranda come into bloom, she remembered her friends: Robin Ordell who was posthumously awarded the Distinguished Flying Cross, and Damien Parer who let Australians at home see how it was on the frontlines in Libya, Greece, Syria, and finally on the island of Peleliu—where he was killed by Japanese machine-gun fire, falling, camera in hand.

———

IN JANUARY 1946, LAWRIE Brooks, fresh out of the army and the newest jewel in the crown of the Colgate-Palmolive Radio Unit, was given an appointment with Miss Gloria van Boss. That day, as he reached across the desk to shake her outstretched hand, he had little idea that he was being hauled to safety.

'Come on in, sit down', my mother would call from her office to the comedians, musicians, comperes, actors and singers as they made their way to the sound studios. 'Talk to me, tell me your news, what's been going on . . . Let me make you famous.'

It was no line. She was astute at knowing what would enter-tain, what would make a headline. And she could spot raw talent. She discovered Willie Fennell, a natural comedian, at a local party and set the radio operator from the Rose Bay flying base on a course that would enable him to become one of the station's stars. She was instrumental in proposing Harry Grif-fiths, her office boy, as straight man to comedian Dick Bentley. This led to an offer from Roy 'Mo' Rene, who made Griffiths a household name with the phrase, 'Cop this, young Harry'.

Everything was of interest to her. If she heard Dick Bentley, the comedian made famous on the BBC's *Take it from Here*, had received a great new joke in a letter from the UK, she would hunt him down to use it in a press release. If Peggy Brooks, the singer, was involved in an interesting new liaison, she'd put the word out: 'Get her to ring me, I want to talk to her.'

Everyone ended up in my mother's office, which was an open house every afternoon when she put on a tea party complete with scones. People came for her company because, as Harry Griffiths recalled, she was 'quick' and 'bright' and, like her mentor and friend Jack Davey, she was 'a doer'. They all knew if they wanted to see their name in the press that she, the Publicity Officer of the most successful radio entertainment unit in Australia, was the woman who could put it there.

While she immediately thought Lawrie Brooks handsome, and while she was beguiled by his softly spoken voice that could rise to the heights of a great tenor, she couldn't have guessed that within eight months she would be part of the publicity herself. There she would stand, arm in arm with this man in the middle of Hyde Park, having her photograph taken for a full-page story for the magazine, *Radio Pictorial*. Under the picture, in big bold type, would run the word 'Engaged'.

On that winter day in August, as they beamed into the camera, they looked every inch the Hollywood couple: she elegant, with Lauren Bacall lacquered pageboy hair, tailored suit, fur muff and Katharine Hepburn brogues, while he sported a Bogart-type wide-shouldered double-breasted suit, with a silk handkerchief flying from its pocket and his ubiquitous Noel Coward cigarette-holder in his hand.

How did they arrive at that moment? A decade before, not only were they hemispheres apart but planets spinning in entirely different orbits. While he'd been gambling, carousing, crashing cars and breaking the marriage laws, she had been making her debut in virginal white as 'one of twenty young lovely maidens' being presented to His Excellency, the Governor Lord Wake-hurst at the Christian Brothers College Ball. And while he was drinking the nights away, propping up the bars of Kings Cross with the boys in the band, she was being written up in the social pages as 'well known in Eastern Suburbs A.U.P. (Australian United Party) younger set circles' and, on the occasion of her twenty-first birthday, being 'entertained at the home of her grandparents in the quiet country town of Boorowa'.

When Lawrie Brooks took up his new position with Colgate-Palmolive, the glitzy girls in the unit vied to catch the attention of the singer, whose outstretched arms when he sang seemed to reach out only to them. However, he told me that it was Miss van Boss, walking down the office corridor in her sharply cut, form-hugging suit, who triggered his attention. That, and the fact he found it intriguing that in his personal Miss World contest, he had never dated a Dutch girl before. After a series of dates, and by the time he learned her surname was adopted, Lawrie was happy to know he never would.

My father said he never 'wolfed', by which he meant he waited for the 'gal' to make the first move. He said it was 'some twisted sense of romantic gallantry'. But when it came to my mother, he was required to make the first move. He told me once that when he watched her leaning over the cot of her baby niece, tucking her in to sleep, he knew then that she was the one.

I am supposing that through the shadows of that dimly lit room, he saw a composite of his ideal woman: something of the grandmother who had loved and nurtured him; something of the aunt who had championed him; but also, inch by attractive inch, someone who was more of a woman than any he had encountered throughout his wild years. She was the one who would sustain both his head and his heart, and who would be steadfast to the point of walking the plank. She, he knew instinctively, was the one who could save him.

And so, just months after meeting her, he wrote to his Aunt Bess (the one he named in his passport to be contacted in case of emergency, instead of his mother). He described his loneliness and his hope of ending it with a new love. Bess, perhaps by this time immune to her nephew's betrothals, simply responded with a one-liner before getting onto three pages of other business: *'About the gal, I hardly know what to say.'*

He knew exactly what to say. Shortly after receiving his aunt's brush-off response, he proposed on the tram trundling up New South Head Road to Vaucluse. He prefaced his troth by revealing his long history of desertion, loss, bad timing, disastrous love affairs and miserable divorces. It took the entire journey from the city to my mother's home to do that. In the end, all she could do was laugh at the domino fall of blackness and then agree to change his luck from bad to good by saying 'yes'.

Many of his friends warned her off him. He wasn't as easy as the songs he sung. He had, by now, using boxing skills taught to him by Stanley in the orange grove, lost a good deal of his eyebrows in skirmishes. An army mate described him as: 'A sweet-singing American, very easy to get on with except when "over-charged" . . .'

He believed she would be his 'for life, the perfect wife', the one who would settle him down. He would marry for the fourth and last time to a woman he saw as 'an innocent but interesting-eyed beauty ... standoffish ... let's-keep-it-down-to-earth ... not gaudy but chic ... intelligent and wise and yet a simple kid ... a gal to stick through thick and thin and not really know there were any other men in the world.'

When their engagement party was thrown at my mother's parents' house on a Sunday in July 1946, the neighbours were treated to the sight of Australia's best-known entertainers wandering along under the water tower in Black Street. After the toasts, in keeping with the tradition of party pieces when performers got together, singers sang, musicians played, actors recited and laughter rocked the street. Dick Bentley, Hal Lashwood, Willie Fennell, Roy 'Mo' Rene, Jack Davey, Rex 'Wacka' Dawes all did their best to out-fun and out-pun each other with skits and gags. These were people my mother had worked with since she was a young girl and they had come because they loved her. Many were cohorts of my father—musicians and those with the particular bond formed on stages big and small, in dressing rooms and late-night bars.

The man who had grown up without parents, who had lived most of his adult life in hotels, must now have felt like a Russian doll—inside a family, inside a family, inside a family—accepted and embraced by his showbiz colleagues, his army mates, and now his wife's relatives and friends. It was something he could never have imagined as a stranger on Australia's shore when he first shared a stage with 'Mo'. 'Life suddenly seemed gloriously amber' is how he put it, perhaps as he raised a glass of whiskey reflecting the city's golden light.

He wrote a song to his two new loves, Sydney and his Australian girl. Underneath the boast of the ladies' man, you hear the relief at the promise of leaving his past behind—the hope that at last he had been stopped in his wandering tracks.

On Park Avenue, the Bronx or the 'Loo,
Romantic Madrid or a height in Peru,
A pretty girl is where you find her.
I think you'll agree,
But hear this history:
I've got a gal in Woolloomooloo
I've got a gal in Timbuctoo
I've got a blonde hair beauty
She's a cutie
That's the one I met back in old Purdue
Yes, there's the gal in Woolloomooloo
Another hon in Honolulu
And there's a dark eye lassie, very classy
That's the one I left back in Kalamazoo
I've been around the world you can bet
About as far as one guy could get
They said that travel would unravel all of my cares
Travel's only landed me in tangled affairs
But here's a secret I'll tell you
And you can bet it's every word true
The gal that's got me guessin'
I'm confessin'
Is the gal in Woolloomooloo.

She's no and yesin'
The gal in Woolloomooloo.

After she accepted his proposal, there was no guessing how she felt. She was 'crazy' about him: his *'walk ... speaking voice ... singing voice ... smile ... laugh.'* She scrawls this, along with *'I love you'*, a dozen times in black ink, as a PS in the margins of a typed letter sent to him while he was on an interstate tour. They had known each other for six months, long enough for him to be calling her parents 'Mum and Dad'. But, on the other hand, long enough for him to warn her: '. . . with your head so far in the clouds of romance I think you can't see me properly.'

Yet, she saw perfectly clearly. Abandonment was something she recognised up close. And under the layers of Lawrie, Lawrence, Bob, Robert, Buster she could see a heart to repair, to nurture, someone on whom to lavish her hope—someone who needed what she had always wanted, the fortress of a picket fence.

Chapter Ten

AFTER AN ENGAGEMENT OF just four months (war-weary people didn't dawdle), my mother quit her highly paid job as Publicity Officer to become Mrs Brooks and a housewife with home duties. It was the expected thing to do. The engagement was probably longer than planned simply because accommodation was hard to find. Not only were places to rent scarce in the post-war period, but in 1946 there would have been very few people who hadn't heard of my father, arguably the top Australian singer of popular songs in the 1940s and early 1950s. In the case of house hunting, this proved to be a problem. One prospective landlord summed up his concern with showbiz folk: 'There would be too many sherry parties.' Finally, they found a flat in Neutral Bay, just up the hill from the ferry. In those busy years, while Lawrie Brooks was under exclusive contract with Colgate-Palmolive, it definitely was party time.

News of my arrival—I was due in December 1947—saw them packing, crossing the Bridge and heading for larger accommodation in Coogee. The three-storeyed, bay-windowed block of flats sat opposite a green reserve and was one street up from the ocean. Courtesy of the colicky baby they carried home from St Margaret's Hospital, my parents became familiar with every inch of their beautiful surroundings. To soothe my tears the pram would be pushed around and up and down, day and night. If still defeated by my wailing, they'd resort to hailing a taxi and riding aimlessly around until the heavier wheels swayed me off to sleep. I can't imagine when my father slept, given he was broadcasting on radio stations countrywide, recording, and singing on stages in Sydney and interstate with the likes of Chips Rafferty and Peter Finch on the same bill.

—

Darleen Penelope Cecilia Brooks
Sits in her cot and reads her books
Sits in her cot while her mother cooks
Darleen Penelope Cecilia Brooks.

My father penned this ditty around my mouthful of a name. It had expanded at the baptismal font in St Brigid's Church, Coogee, when the priest informed my parents there could be no christening without a saint's name: the American Darleen and the pagan Penelope just wouldn't do. When my father immediately came up with the name Cecilia, the patron saint of music, the holy water was duly poured.

By the time he recited this rhyme to me my parents had bought and sold their first house in Marrickville and, while completing complicated negotiations on their new home, were living in rented rooms in Bellevue Hill. There we shared a Californian bungalow in Fairweather Street with Mrs Redstone, the widow who owned it. I slept just outside my parents' bedroom on a built-in veranda, in a cot with pull-down rails that allowed escape. Early morning, I'd entertain myself while they slept by raiding the biscuit packet and seeing how neatly my teeth could wind their way around the clock stamped into the Arnott's shortbread.

In between my circumnavigation of the biscuit, I'd explore the world in my Little Golden Books where everything, despite problems, always worked out well. I adored the pretty face of Nurse Nancy and the fluffy three little kittens that lost their mittens and the clever parents in *Fix It, Please*, who patched up any disaster for their rosy-cheeked children by application of either a Band-Aid or glue.

From the vantage point of my cot situated by the back door, I'd sometimes wake in the night to see my father softly enter and watch as he tiptoed through moonlight into the bedroom. I didn't know it then, but he was returning at all hours of the night after performing in a show or a radio broadcast. My father was attentive, always affectionate, but as he now worked both night and day I saw him fleetingly.

My mother created worlds for me in the small back garden. From leaves and sticks she fashioned outrageous hats and became a solicitous milliner, tempting me with her various creations.

Or, changing roles, I would be the storekeeper serving a snooty woman by the name of Mrs Kafoops, who hailed from Emu Plains and spoke as though a clothes peg was pinching her nose. In her faux British accent, she insisted on purchasing 'a dozen double damask dinner napkins'. Nothing could steer her off her course, but that was the game—to persuade her to change her order. 'Oh, I'm so sorry, Mrs Kafoops, we are out of a dozen double damask dinner napkins. May I interest you in four cotton serviettes?' The speed of the bantering would accelerate until our tongues tripped up.

A highlight of my day would be hearing the baker's horse clip-clopping down Fairweather Street. Pennies would be pressed into my hand and I'd race down the dark lane at the side of the house into the sunny view of a beautiful horse, whose earthy scent mingled with the still-warm baked bread stacked in the back of the wooden cart. Having handed over my money, I'd watch as the baker tore a loaf in half, always hoping the larger half would be the one handed to me. When luck was mine, the feet that had flown to the cart now dawdled, allowing me time to nibble pieces of the loaf while trying to convince myself I was helping to even it up. Nothing was ever said until one day I lost all restraint, and my mother had to cut most of the loaf before she could find a slice without a gaping hole.

I think we spent a lot of time in the garden because Mrs Redstone, our landlady, was constantly policing my mother in the shared house. We had instructions not to do this, not to touch that. However, permission to enter the hallowed front room was always granted to listen to the radio and hear my father sing.

Gloria Brooks, wife of singer Lawrie Brooks, was listening to a special radio piece the other night. Three-year old daughter Darleen kept up a non-stop chatter. 'Don't keep on talking, darling, Mummy's listening to the radio,' said Gloria. Darleen looked dismayed. Flinging herself and her doll on the carpet, she said, 'I CAN'T stop talking: I'm playing ladies, and ladies never stop talking.'

This is a story my mother must have related to one of her journalist friends because, *voilà*, when I was sitting in the NSW State Library researching for this book, I found myself back in Mrs Redstone's living room in a column on the front page of *The Sun*. I don't recall that scene, but the lyrics of the songs I heard on that radio still play in my head. 'Autumn Leaves', wistful and melancholic, painted a picture of a summer romance and parted lovers. And my father singing 'Old Man River', using the cadence of a slave planting his 'taters' and a different grammar, telling me that 'dem dat plants 'em is soon forgotten', translated into a plea for freedom. It was one way to learn rhythm and rhyme and to glimpse a world outside the safety of cot rails.

But if any song seals the memory of that house it's 'When the Red, Red Robin Comes Bob, Bob, Bobbin' Along'. As a special treat, I could choose a tube on which was rolled perforated paper that magically held the music for the pianola. Because my legs couldn't reach the floor, the only way I could make the ghostly piano keys move was by pushing the pedals up and down with my hands.

It must have been the excitement of having my father at home one particular day, because I clearly remember how the sun streaked through the window onto the floral carpet while I made the music for him and he stood in the doorway smiling and we all sang about laughter, love and happiness.

I had no playmates apart from my mother, and as a result I was treated like an adult. So much so that, after I was accepted into the local pre-school kindergarten, I walked up to the teacher and precociously asked, 'Could you keep the children quiet?'

The Latimer kindergarten was newly built. A symbol of fresh beginnings, it was full of the progeny of war refugees, hopeful migrants and demobbed soldiers. There were lockers with individual symbols like an elephant or an umbrella, shiny and colourful and printed on various objects, including daybeds that folded out for afternoon naps. I was enthralled by the newness of it all, the smell of the fresh wood and paint, and the fact it was a world built just for children.

The building still stands, up the road from Cooper's Corner on New South Head Road in Double Bay. Back when my mother and I walked there (most of the way I'd be pushed in my pram) except for an occasional car or tram, we could almost whisper and still be heard. It was a slower, quieter world at the beginning of the 1950s, with just one in ten families owning a car, a car that would take its sweet time shifting through the gears. Back then, people walked, and my mother more than most. It was two kilometres down to the kindergarten and two kilometres back up that high hill. She did this twice a day.

My bad behaviour eventually saved her the trip—I was expelled. My dislike of afternoon naps prompted me to such boredom that I'd wake the other children when the teacher's head was turned. If they were heavy sleepers I remember resorting to a gentle pinch. 'Disruptive' was the word they used—a precursor to another 'D' for 'Dreamer' that defined my 'D' for 'Dismal' school career.

It was on one of these walks I learned that my mother didn't hold sway over the planet. We had stopped on Bellevue Road to speak to an acquaintance. 'I'm on my way to vote out the rats,' said my mother. The word 'rats' galvanised my attention. I had no idea she was referring to Communists. It was September 1951 and Robert Menzies had called for a referendum to ban the Communist Party in Australia. At my mother's pronouncement the woman lost her smile and, fuelled by righteous indignation, informed anyone within earshot that she was returning from the polling booth, having voted to the contrary. Witnessing my mother's discomfort, to hear her being challenged, was shocking. Worse still was the realisation that I was helpless to rescue her.

Menzies' referendum failed to win national support but there are several reasons that may have influenced my democratic mother's support of his doomed attempt. It's possible that my grandmother's politics were a factor because she had supported Menzies since the inception of the Liberal Party in 1944. During the referendum, she was spreading Liberal propaganda song sheets with the refrain: 'The only Red we want, Is the Red we've got, In the old Red, White and Blue.' My mother's mother was such a force in the Liberal Party's Women's Group that the local federal member of parliament at one time wrote to her, in his capacity as Minister for Defence, thanking her for her personal contribution to his successful campaign.

But perhaps the overriding reason for my mother wanting to eradicate the Communist Party was linked to my father. While he was being called a 'Yank', he was also being called a 'Commo'. Such name-calling had its origin in American politics: President Truman in 1947 had begun a witch-hunt by screening federal employees for any sign of Communist sympathisers. After that, when the Communist Party won the Civil War in China in 1949, paranoia took serious hold, ushering in the era of McCarthyism. The Un-American Activities Committee identified the entertainment industry in particular as a hot bed of Communist sympathisers and promoters, and ran campaigns that pointed directly to the source of the Russian menace: 'Don't patronize Reds!!! You can drive the Reds out of television, radio and Hollywood.'

Australia quickly followed suit, and my father became an easy target. He ticked many of the McCarthy boxes: he was an American entertainer; after the war he sang at fundraisers, such as 'Food for Britain', a charity that in 1947 was associated with the Communist Party; and he believed in the absolute necessity of trade unions. Despite being firmly entrenched as a member of Actors Equity, first as a Councillor, later as Senior Vice President and then as acting Federal President, by April 1953 he resigned. I remember my mother later spoke of blackballing. A whisper here, a doubt sown there, and it was easy to become targeted by a rival performer.

My father survived. He had spent his life practising that particular skill.

Chapter Eleven

DESPITE HIS FAME, the stage wasn't my father's natural habitat. He disguised a great shyness and vulnerability under his stand-and-deliver persona; listening to his old recordings now, I marvel at the courage it must have taken, not only as the centre of attention, but to reach seemingly impossibly high notes as he performed live to air and in front of large audiences. There was another hurdle—his constant worry that he would forget his lyrics. Like a juggler or a trapeze artist or an actor with a Shakespearean soliloquy, he had to trust his skill and take the leap. After the shows, to calm his nerves, to douse the adrenaline, to be one of the boys, my father drank. Working at Sydney's most celebrated nightclubs of this era, including Prince's and The Roosevelt, did nothing to discourage this habit.

Rolling home in the early hours of the morning wasn't a life for a married man with a small child. He was a blackout drunk who, when sober and returned to his usual gentle self, had no memory of the man he had been the night before. There was one such night that my mother found too painful to detail. All I know is that her brother arrived to scoop her up and take us to his home for safekeeping.

Perhaps that was the day my father resolved to avoid the wild drinking, to gain some equilibrium, to find once again the grace and comfort of his grandparents' home—to determine to hold onto his family. Certainly it was around this time that he secured a mortgage. To do this meant taking a permanent job and he chose one just a step away from his first desired profession. He became a proof-reader, the one in charge of correcting the errors of the journalist and typesetters. It was a popular occupation among his musician mates because it allowed flexible hours to fit around musical and recording engagements.

They moved from the rented flat in Coogee to the quiet cul-de-sac of Pilgrim Avenue, Marrickville and there they straddled worlds. My father had lived out of hotels most of his theatrical working life, and my mother had treated her radio station like home. They were used to microphones, not calling over the backyard fence. But we stayed in Pilgrim Avenue long enough for my father to build a swing and for me to be pushed in it.

Then came an opportunity to sell the Marrickville house and buy a pair of Victorian terraces in Bland Street, Ashfield that had fallen into disrepair. The current tenants were paying next to nought for rent, which meant the property was going at a bargain price. My parents were willing to wait for their leases to expire and then planned to restore the houses and rent out rooms. That way, they reasoned, the mortgage would be paid off with speed.

———

But when possession of the Ashfield property became protracted, rather than wait any longer within the confines of Mrs Redstone's bungalow, we travelled some 60 kilometres down the south coast to live in Stanwell Park.

In 1952, it was a wild green amphitheatre trimmed by ocean and a long ribbon of sand. From the beach a valley spread, winding towards cliffs bounded by ferns growing under high gums. A few small iron-roofed houses lay under a wide sky. Just as the ranch house in an orange orchard on the outskirts of Fullerton was the golden memory of my father's youth, Stanwell Park would become the shining memory of mine.

My days started to all sorts of alarms: some to a stormy ocean, others to kookaburras calling up the light—but always there would be the whistle of the train, like the final bell before the curtain went up. Immediately following that whistle, around the curve of the southern cliff, came a bouquet of cloudy steam. It was a starter's flag, announcing my father's daily race to the station to catch the one and only daily passenger train into Sydney.

It became a ritual, a hurried kiss for 'his girls' and then we'd watch as he disappeared through the tangle of undergrowth and began his run to the station. We would stand together, anxiously measuring the slow gait of the train to his sprint and worrying if this would be the day he wouldn't make it. When a large white handkerchief invariably fluttered from a carriage window, my mother's face shone, as if he'd won an Olympic gold.

Our world was as sure and regulated as a toy train running on its circular track. During the time we lived in that rented house on top of the ocean, I don't remember any arguments between my parents. If my father was to make the train home, there was no time for drinks with the boys after work and no chance for evening singing engagements. We never heard the slurred excuses that were to become familiar over the next couple of decades: the 'unexpected celebration,' the 'needy mate'. He was always on that train.

He was the frontier man, literally bringing home the bacon. He would walk back up the hill at the end of the day carrying shiny white packages wrapped by the butcher and brown paper bags with vegetables that weren't available among the basics at Stanwell Park's one and only store.

The house was simple: fibro, boxy, with a front screen door that opened onto a mosquito-netted veranda. I loved every plain inch of it. Electricity was conducted by larger-than-life telegraph poles, but there was no mains water or sewerage. Water came from a rain tank, heat from the wood stove and an open fireplace, and milk from the inherited cow that came with the rented property.

On our first morning, the needy cow stuck her head through my parents' bedroom window and mooed them awake. I remember them in their silk dressing gowns, laughing as if they were at a party while they circled the cow, looking at her swollen udder like two country hicks gazing up at a skyscraper.

Robert 'Buster' Cutter

'Buster' under the watchful eye of his loving grandmother, Blanche Conkey.

'Buster' greeting a friend on the once green and pleasant streets of his hometown of Santa Maria.

On entering Fullerton High School.

The local newspaper reported: 'Robert Cutter, Fullerton writer . . . has just disposed of two stories to a magazine. He plans to make writing his life work.' He is twenty-one.

Bob Cutter's first radio show on KGU in Honolulu. He wrote, produced and sang under the title 'Mr Velvet'.

Katharine Smith arrives in Honolulu in 1932 and is greeted at the wharf by Bob Cutter carrying a ring.

Honolulu in the 1930s—when the Royal Hawaiian Hotel truly ruled Waikiki.

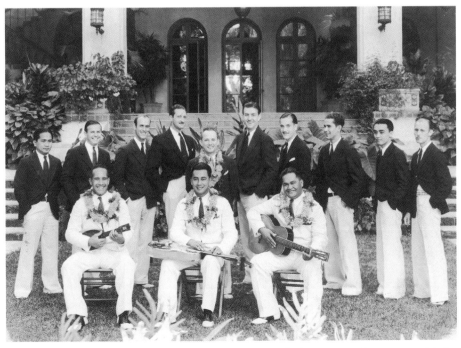

Outside the Royal Hawaiian Hotel, 1935. My father is standing second left.

In 1935 Bob Cutter was Honolulu's favourite soloist.

Rubey Bacon. She would become Rubey Cutter illegally in 1936 and legally in 1937.

The splendour of the Biltmore Bowl where my father sang at the
8th Academy Awards.

Musicians playing softball: the singer stands behind the bandleader,
Jay Whidden, who is pitching.

Bob Cutter arrives in Australia as Lawrence Brooks, and is billed at Melbourne's Palais de Danse as the 'Young American' singer.

Lawrence Brooks performing in his first Tivoli season, 1938. He stands centre stage in white.

The 2nd Australian Imperial Force Entertainment Unit in the Middle East.

Lawrie Brooks with Tex Morton: both singers performed with the
Jim Davidson Orchestra, pre-war and later for the troops.

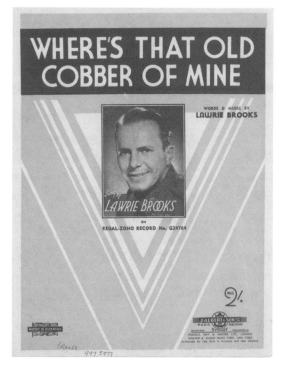

Sheet music for a song
composed by my father in
memory of fallen comrades.
It was one of the most
requested songs among
the troops fighting in
New Guinea.

Lawrie Brooks, back from the war, surrounded by showgirls once again.

Lawrie Brooks at
thirty-nine.

My mother, Gloria van Boss, aged twenty-four and hosting her own radio
program on 2CA Canberra.

'ENGAGED' the magazine headline shouted out in 1946.

'You're the reason I sing' my father wrote to his new bride, Gloria Brooks.

Morneen (to be shortened to Miki), the first of his three daughters.

A forty-eight-year-old Lawrie Brooks delighting in his daughter Geraldine, his 'late in life surprise'.

When asked by a journalist in 1947, the year of my birth, if he would return to America, my father said: 'My little baby girl would regret leaving her native land.'

Stanwell Park: my playground came complete with a cat, a dog, a cow, a swing, paddocks and a lagoon.

A proud father with his daughters as they head off for their first day at a new school. Concord, January 1961.

Sisters, mirroring each other's delight, as we listen to my son singing. Christmas Day 2000.

A bucket was found, a stool and, despite lame advice from my father, eventually necessity won the day and my mother began her career as a milkmaid.

There was a line-and-post fence running around our large front lawn, but it failed to define much for me. My swing (the second of five my father would build) was perched on a high point of headland above the beach not far from where the pioneer of flight, Lawrence Hargrave, first took to the air. I can't imagine Hargrave felt any more excitement than I did as I flew, pushing myself higher and higher on that swing, until all that was spread out under my airborne feet I claimed as mine.

Weeks would pass and our only visitor was the dunny man. Perhaps he never smelled sweeter than the day my mother treated him to her solution for a hygienic outhouse. Manoeuvring the door with her foot, she didn't have time to notice the poor man inside about to retrieve the can. By the time she did, he had been sluiced with the contents of a steaming hot bucket of water, doused with disinfectant.

Whatever spare time she had, after cleaning the house, or washing in the wood-fired copper, or baking on the old iron range, my mother gave to me. There were books and games and long walks, exploring life in the rock pools and plants in the paddocks.

On 4 September 1952, we were out on a treasure hunt searching for freesias that glinted orange, yellow and red, fragrant in the spring grasses. I was clutching a small bunch when, for some inexplicable reason, we both looked up towards the cliff road. The narrow two-lane road cut into the rugged coastline, delivering sightseers and weekenders willing to make the winding coastal drive down from Sydney. To the left and hundreds of metres below, the sea smashed against the foot of the cliffs. To the right, a jagged escarpment lurched sharply skywards. Along the coast road, signposts repeated the message: *Beware of Falling Rocks*. There should have been another warning sign before the bend to Stanwell Park: *Beware of the View*.

What happened in the car as it took the turn? Maybe the grandparents, the boy, the girl and their mother were all struck by the clamour of crystal sparking off the sea. Perhaps the boy shouted, 'Look!' and they all leaned towards the view. Experts surmised that the brake might have been mistaken for the accelerator. Whatever happened in that little black Ford, in a heartbeat the world lost its footing—earth became sky, sky became sea.

To my eyes it happened in slow motion. The car, crawling along, stopped just after the turn. Then easily, almost gracefully, it lifted on its side. For a brief moment, it seemed it would correct itself; but then the safety fence shattered and, amid a hail of splintered white wood, the car fell. Noise filled the valley as metal collided with earth, rocks, timber. The newspaper reported it fell over 90 metres before finally being braced by a tree. Each time the car rolled and bounced there was a deep hollow thud. I'd hear its deathly echo years later in London, when an IRA bomb exploded with the same gut-thudding emptiness.

Although the tragedy was happening far from us, my not-yet-five-year-old brain was convinced that the tree-crushing car would keep falling until it fell on me (a car crashing through the sky, like the planes descending into Mascot). Shocked as she must have been, my mother remained calm as she gathered me up and deposited me with the nearest neighbour. Then she ran towards the accident. On the lower face of the cliff she found the boy. His grandfather lay dead beside his sister further up the hill; his mother lay bleeding and unconscious in the upturned car, and his grandmother lay mutilated and dead behind it. While waiting for the rescue team she cradled the boy, distracting him, asking what he would like as a reward for being brave, whispering she would get it for him. He said he wanted a drum.

Later, on the day my mother left on the long journey to visit the boy in hospital, she told me that promises must be kept. When she arrived, medical staff informed her he hadn't uttered a sound since the accident. When she handed him the promised drum, he screamed, then wept to remember.

Not even that terrible accident marred those magical months for me. Neither did falling face first into a blackberry patch, or the snake, wrestled out from under one of those patches, left draped over our fence like a long fat skipping rope. To this day, I search in vain for blackberries with the same intense sun-baked sweetness, for the rich perfume of those wild freesias and the scent of chocolate cake cooking in a wood-fired oven.

The only anxiety I felt that whole time was watching my father's worried face as he tapped to gauge the meagre amount of water remaining in the tank during the long dry summer. It was a summer so hot that on one particular day my last attempt to get relief was to lie spread-eagled under the kitchen table, the only place I could find shade.

I recall one such 'stinker' (my mother's description for heatwave days) when the beach was crowded with weekend day-trippers. A family had spread out next to us and were enjoying a vast picnic. Among their feast they unpacked a huge watermelon, something we would never find in the general store. My mother must have been watching my face as the refreshing scent floated on the salt dry air and observed my longing as I followed every crunch, every drip of coolness, every sweet pink rivulet snaking down chins and over swimsuits. When she stood up, pocketing her pride, and walked over to ask those strangers if they could possibly spare a slice for me, I realised my mother loved me to the point of embarrassment.

If my father had been sitting on the beach that day, to ask if he would have made such a request is irrelevant—he would have been oblivious. On the other hand, he spent months patiently teaching me to swim in the safety of the lagoon. I managed to swim underwater, but it would be a few more years until I'd learn the Australian crawl. This small success drew his enormous approval. It was important to him, just as the relinquishing of my nightlight seemed to be. I remember thinking his reaction strange when I asked him to close the door and leave me in darkness. His pleasure seemed far too large for such a small request. As I lay listening to the call of an animal out in the pitch blackness, I heard him boast to my mother: 'Who would have thought she'd have no fear of the dark way out here, in the middle of nowhere.'

Only while reading through his old letters for this book, did I learn that as a teenager he harboured a terrible fear of the night. It came as a revelation because I can't remember a time when I felt my father was afraid of anything. But now, weighing the circumstances, I begin to understand why. As a child, so much that he had depended on and loved had deserted him or been lost forever: his brother a constant ghost, his parents gone, the death of all his pets—Silver the cat drowned in a rain barrel while he was confined to his room with measles, and the family border collie, Prince, was run down by Dr Brown's car.

Perhaps as a small boy he believed it had all been his fault for being sick. Perhaps he imagined that his parents would have kept him and stayed together if he hadn't been so ill, and that perhaps his brother's death occurred because they were so busy looking after him—the newborn—rather than Ronald. As he grew to adolescence all that stood between him and an unstable and dangerous world were his aged grandparents.

By the time he reached his teens, this loss was given shape in the Los Angeles Forest Lawn cemetery. Fred, a family friend, had enlisted my father's help, asking him to drive down to Los Angeles with him to pick up an exhumation. When they arrived, Fred cajoled the reluctant attendants to open the coffin. He then forced the teenager to look inside the casket. In the box lay a shrunken body covered in a cobwebby mould with hair visibly grown while the flesh had collapsed into decay. For years after, in my father's nightmares a dead body—sometimes of a man, sometimes of a woman—would rise and sit up in an open coffin.

In his graduating year at Fullerton High School, he wrote a poem entitled 'Vitality at Ebb'. When it was published in the school paper, *The Pleiades*, his fellow students would have had no idea how confessional this work was—how dread lived behind his clear blue eyes and shadowed his beautiful smile.

> *Oh God!*
> *Protect me from this spirit of the night*
> *Which haunts my sleep;*
> *Attacks me*
> *Under cover of darkness*
> *Blacker than the Styx,*
> *And fills me with a nameless dread;*
> *Chills me so that I cannot move,*
> *Stops my breath,*
> *Tugs at my heart,*
> *Binds my soul—*
> *Oh God!*
> *Spare me this visitation from the dead.*

When the time came and the legalities of the Ashfield terrace were finally completed, the move back to Sydney appeared to be met by my parents with confused enthusiasm. I think they had planned the interlude as a picnic, a long camp out; but when they announced the moving date, their voices had the same artificial jolliness conjured up for a trip to the doctor or dentist. They were trying to bolster their own spirits as well as mine. The time spent in Stanwell Park my mother would tell me decades later, had been one of the happiest of their lives.

When we returned to the enclosure of the city, there were wild reversals. I felt more alone in my crowded school playground than in the emptiness of the country. Between his numerous singing engagements, writing commitments, working nights as a proof-reader and taking on the job of renovating the terrace houses, my father spent less time with me.

On occasions my parents quarrelled. I have no recollection as to why, or even if they were arguments of any significance. I do remember one evening, as I listened to their angry voices, calmly thinking that perhaps they would be happier apart and that I should love them both equally and just as much. I could cope with this. But at my convent school the nuns' dedication to the deliberation of sin and all its fiery punishment, created problems that seemed unsolvable to me. I became anxious in the late afternoon, knowing that the sun would soon be going down, and for several years I suffered a terror of the dark to rival that of my father's when he was young.

Chapter Twelve

WHEN MY FATHER FIRST sighted those Ashfield terraces, he must have felt a connection. He would have been drawn to the verandas with the decorative wooden trim, which resembled the fretwork on the porch of the house that he grew up in Chapel Street, Santa Maria, California. The generous dimensions, sash windows, the crafted detailing—all would have carried the comforting feeling of his grandparents' home. 'They loved me,' he once told me. 'They really loved me.'

Like Goldilocks, I would try almost every room in both houses as we shifted around so as to accommodate various tenants. I remember an interesting parade: people in limbo, in transit, some scrambling to make new lives after the war. The only permanent residents were two elderly sisters who my parents had agreed to inherit with the house.

To me, not yet six years old, Miss Martin and Mrs Paterson appeared as old as all history. Their rooms were sunless, shrouded in heavy drapes with crocheted cloths and yellowing lace covering dark brown furniture. This crowded, dimly lit place smelled almost as musty as they did, but their patient kindness to me, and later to my sister, made them our friends. There was a Welsh woman with a shawl-draped armchair, who seemed lonely, disaffected. She had brought with her a delicate, well-polished, antique spinning wheel from across the sea and when I expressed interest, she informed me in a lilting accent of its history and the home she had left behind. As I listened, I had the sense that she felt she was dealing with a child who, by living in such a new and far-flung country, would never be able to comprehend a civilised world.

One of the other residents spoke with a cutting accent. He was an Atlas—tall, tanned, blond, electrically blue-eyed— a divorcée with an imposing, dismissive manner. He exposed a major fault-line in my usually empathetic father, who held a lifelong prejudice against all Germans. The man's name was Lutz, and I'd hear my father muttering 'Lutzie' and expressing doubts about the man's whereabouts during the war. One day, looking to play with his daughter who would occasionally visit, I ventured into the Lutz kitchen. At the sight of him across the black and white linoleum floor I stood gaping and confused: I had never seen a naked person standing at a kitchen sink before. Storming across the room, grabbing up his bath towel and snapping it angrily around his waist, he looked down at me and spat out, 'Bloody zoo!' With that pronouncement, I fled.

There were two young women I adored. They were always sweet to me as I sat on their kitchen step and watched them prepare dinner; they would chat away, slicing and giggling, chopping and laughing. I remember longing to be them, to the extent that once or twice I snuck into their kitchen while they were at work and attempted to sound and look like them as I busily moved around, chattering away while I emptied spoonfuls of barley and sugar into saucepans, adding cold water and stirring furiously, pretending to cook. I blush now, wondering what they must have thought coming home to a kitchen that had so obviously been burgled, finding grains of sugar and barley about the place. I can't begin to imagine the trouble I would have been in if my mother had discovered my attempt at a double life.

And there was a 'traveller'—a salesman, who at first received my mother's approval because of a photograph he displayed in his room of his younger self as an altar boy. However, his fall from grace was swift. She told me years later that she had seen him splayed across the grass in the local park, displaying affection towards a woman in a manner to scare the horses.

My father would repair and paint the rooms and my mother would clean them. It must have been hard work but they never complained. We lived simply as we shuffled furniture around the houses: a table and chairs, beds, a wardrobe, a lounge and an easy chair. Possessions didn't mean anything to my parents, either then, or in all the years to follow. The only thing they ever aspired to owning was a piece of paper from the bank saying that the mortgage was cleared, and they owned their home and the soil on which it stood: unassailable, no matter which way the world turned.

Each terrace house originally stood as four high-ceilinged, spacious rooms—two up and two down. But, by the time we arrived, haphazard extensions of bedrooms, kitchens and bathrooms had attached themselves like barnacles to the backs and sides of the handsome houses. As a result, my various bedrooms suffered from a lack of airflow, with the original exterior window opening onto an interior extension. In the winter, it meant damp and mildew and, in the summer, breezeless heat. Nevertheless, fuelled by fear, I would stoke the furnace of my bedroom by gathering every one of my friends into my bed and under the covers—Big Bear, Small Bear, Felix the Cat, Punch, Betty the doll and White Rabbit (complete with vest and pocket watch). I'd press them to me like armour, hiding behind their stifling wall of protection, sweating and terrified.

My father's final words to me at the end of each day were: 'See you in the morning, when the sun comes up. And even if it doesn't come up, I'll still see you.' I didn't believe him: I never thought I would survive the night. My parents had no idea of the extent of my terror. Following Dr Spock's rules of child rearing, they would sit on the end of my bed and try to reason with me; but I was never permitted to sleep in their bed.

Finally, rather than spending nights drenched in fear, I devised a plan. I would wait until the house became silent and then reach out in the dark for the rug that I had earlier in the day strategically placed at the foot of my bed. Then I'd tiptoe into my parents' room and sleep by their bed, until the first light would wake me and I'd sneak back to my room. They remained oblivious until one morning I missed the sun's alarm and was woken instead by my mother's startled cry. On rising she had narrowly avoided stepping on me. During this time I remember nights that brought a reprieve. I could easily fall asleep in my own bed when the Test Series was being broadcast from England and my father would have the radio on softly, listening throughout the night. To this day, to hear a cricket commentary is to hear a lullaby.

—

IF YOU COULD HAVE looked through the window of my class-room in 1953 during religious instruction, you would have seen long lines of children, aged between five and six, sitting behind brown school desks listening to a black-draped nun. If you'd opened the door to that classroom, you would have walked straight through the gates of Hell. You would have heard the nun instruct us: 'Imagine someone striking a match and holding your finger over the flame.' Looking about the class and satisfied by the frightened engagement of innocent faces, she proceeded: 'Now imagine Bondi Beach and all the grains of sand on Bondi Beach. There would be hundreds and hundreds of millions of grains wouldn't there?' Scarcely able to count without the use of fingers, but liking games of imagination, we nodded. 'Now try to imagine all the grains of sand on all the beaches in all the world.' We scrunched our foreheads, realising we had definitely reached the unimaginable. 'Well,' the Sister of Charity contin-ued, 'that isn't even the beginning of the amount of pain you would feel in the fires of Hell—it will go on forever and ever if you commit a mortal sin.'

Many of my classmates suffered from stuttering and bed-wetting, but my fear didn't manifest itself physically. Trudging home from school that day, and for years afterwards, I would fret over my parents' salvation. It was a mortal sin to miss Mass on Sunday, and a mortal sin to be divorced, and a mortal sin to marry a divorced man. Guilty on all three counts. And I . . . I was a bastard, because my parents' marriage was not recognised in the eyes of the Catholic Church. 'Nothing to worry about, darling,' they would say. 'That's not right,' they would say. But it was only while the sun shone that I believed them.

A vivid nightmare remains. I am racing through the flat of Mrs Paterson and Miss Martin towards the back door. Their dark rooms have turned technicolour red; walls are collapsing and giant fingers of flame chase me. I arrive at the threshold and look up, just as the fiery wooden lintel above the door breaks apart and falls towards me.

———

MY MOTHER OFTEN SPOKE to me about the suffering of her friends in the Japanese war camps—how some were never the same people when they returned home, how after being close to death by starvation, they would flare into anger if their children left food on the plate, and how the grief of losing her young cousin was a loss she always remembered.

Before each Anzac Day, a box that was full of lapel-sized tin hats and various small badges would be delivered to our house and, on the appointed 'Button Day', my mother would head off to join the other 2000-strong volunteers, raising funds for war orphans. They would stand all day in the city, their Legacy trays hanging on a strap from around their necks, displaying the buttons, ranging in prices from sixpence to far grander amounts, to support war orphans. I recall my mother saying it was usually the people who looked like they could afford the least who gave the most.

My father, on the other hand, never spoke of his war experiences to me but I was aware he kept his old mates close, either through letters or get-togethers. He marched on Anzac Day, lent his support by singing at various fundraisers and, whenever we moved house, signing up to the local RSL was one of the first things on his agenda.

One particular scene comes to me as if on celluloid, because it has replayed so faithfully in my head across the years. The three of us are making our way up Bland Street, Ashfield, on our way to catch a train to the city. I am seven-years-old, skipping between my parents as we all hold hands, swinging our arms and singing the lyrics of 'The Wonderful Wizard of Oz'. I am excited because it is my first trip to a city cinema. But, as I look at their faces, mostly I am amazed by their happiness, astounded that they could be so keen on wizards.

What I didn't understand then was that during the war years my father had performed 'Over the Rainbow' to many a grieving audience and my mother had, like so many others, found solace and hope in the lyrics. It was written for the movie *The Wizard of Oz* and confirmed the theme: there was no place like home. It was a place worth fighting for.

So now I think I can imagine where their happiness sprang from—the realisation that they had survived, that they had found and kept each other, built a home and a family. They would call each other 'mummy' and 'daddy', which was confusing to me then. Now I think they were filling in the missing pieces, the empty spaces of absent parents, completing the picture that was denied them in their childhoods, rounding it out. And, for all I know (for it is about the right time) they may have recently discovered that my mother was pregnant again. She, who always longed for children, would have been overjoyed, particularly as she knew that this time her husband was happy at the prospect.

Chapter Thirteen

I REMEMBER THE EXCITEMENT, the flurry, the juggling of rooms, for we needed more space to accommodate the arrival of an important new resident. Our family was expanding.

It was unusual back in the 1950s for a woman in her late thirties to become pregnant, particularly after a hiatus of seven years, and even more unusual for a forty-eight-year-old man to become a father. The maths was lost on me but in the conversations over our front fence I noticed a great deal of interest in the event. My mother tried to turn it into a form of Immaculate Conception, blessing her announcement with the line, 'Darleen's novenas worked', and the women would laugh knowingly while tossing me head-patting smiles. My mother had some months back discussed the possibility of a brother or sister and I was in thrall, so enamoured by the prospect that I attended a series of Masses on top of my novenas in an attempt to seal the deal.

The day my mother began ironing frantically was the day she disappeared into the depths of St Margaret's Hospital, only to emerge a week later with my sister, Geraldine. Feeling almost entirely responsible for her creation, due to my massive amount of prayers, I felt she was mine and I immediately loved her. There she lay, gurgling and with an unusual cry, like a call to prayer, a gentle 'A la . . . a la . . .' Softly at first, but then, if an interested party didn't appear over her crib, the volume and the speed would intensify—'Alla alla alLA ALLA!'—until her demands couldn't be ignored.

She was cute and enormously interesting for several days. Then a yawning disappointment grew as I realised it would be a long wait for a true playmate. She would become that and a great deal more. But, with almost eight years difference between us, our sisterhood wouldn't fully bloom until she was entering her teenage years and I was leaving mine.

Then, around four years later, came another member of our family and rooms were rearranged yet again. My father's widowed mother arrived from the USA, a place I had discovered some years earlier when I was allowed to venture a few doors down to my friend's house—the only home in the entire street with a television—to watch *Disneyland*. I learned then that America was variously known as Adventure Land, Tomorrow Land, Frontier Land and Fantasy Land. By the time my grandmother arrived, it had become Troubled Land, beset with civil rights protestors demanding change.

We were thrilled to welcome Louise, but that didn't last long. The interest we had in her was soon extinguished by the lack of interest she had in us.

'*Louise is ever Louise. I've really been hard-pressed to identify her as my grandmother. She stands on her laurels. I would feel better if she would say I know I've been a crappy grandmother ...*' Miki wrote this to our father. She had suffered from the neglect that seemed to be my American grandmother's calling card. After my father left the USA and sailed for Australia, when Louise could have been a stand-in for Miki's missing father, she was absent. Despite Miki's attempts across the years to make meaningful contact, Louise responded in cold two-paragraph letters and rarely made a personal appearance.

My Australian grandmother, Phyliss, was sweet to her sour. Prime Minister Paul Keating memorably described the love received from his mother and grandmother as feeling as though he'd been 'wrapped in an asbestos suit', and I could totally relate to that. However, when it came to grandmother Louise, if flames had been licking at my feet, I couldn't vouch she'd even consider throwing her evening cocktail over me. 'It's about time for my highball, Bob,' she'd demand of my father every evening as my mother cooked for her.

Louise bore no resemblance to my father: only her blue eyes gave a glimpse of any genetic inheritance. She was as short as she was wide, with comically small feet in contrast to the weight they carried. She sat a lot, played solitaire, and shrugged one shoulder. This physical tic, combined with the downward curve of her mouth, made her appear as if she cared not a jot for the world.

Geraldine and I called her Gran. We were both wide-eyed when she pulled out of her huge trunk, among her crocheted doilies and old lace made by our great-grandmother, a slew of china ornaments. Geraldine, now grown to the height of an occasional table, was perfectly situated for close enjoyment of the knick-knacks but anything she picked up would be met with the stern instruction: 'That is not a plaything.'

There was one unforgettable time we saw a sparkle in her eye, and heard her laugh so delightedly it seemed to make allowance for all kinds of play. She had travelled out to Australia on a steamer and a few days after her arrival two merchant seamen came to visit. Both my sister and I still remember the shock on our parents' faces when the sailors strode into our living room and, instead of offering a polite peck on the cheek, picked her up and flirtatiously spun her around until her skirt flew wide as a circus tent.

Louise had planned on making Australia home. Perhaps she expected to meet her fourth husband, or perhaps she believed my parents' lives would be more glamorous. I do know that she seemed totally unimpressed with Sydney. She was quick to take offence and quick to give it. I'd proudly point out our icons, only to be dismissed with: 'We have bigger and better in the States.' In a letter to Miki, my father reported my reaction: '*Darleen patriotically debunks her America 1st attitudes.*'

My mother, at the end of the 1950s, was still washing in a copper, using a handwringer, and instead of a refrigerator possessed an icebox (the ice delivery man would come bounding down the side lane of our house once a week carrying a back-breaking block of calipered ice, as if it were a briefcase). Never quick to criticise but always excellent at making a point, my mother wrote to Miki: '*Gran doesn't like Australia much, though she tries to be polite . . . she misses the conveniences of the USA. We are so far behind in modern living—but happy yet!*'

Louise and I didn't agree on anything much, and any affection I had for her was lost one night in the kitchen when we went head to head on American Civil Rights. She defended the status quo, protesting she didn't understand what the internal war was all about, arguing some of the 'negroes' she'd known—who worked for her family—were treated 'like family'. When I pressed her on this, she finally admitted she couldn't countenance inviting anyone from her so-called 'family' to the same table to dine.

She stayed, smoking and glued to her card table, for less than a year. In gratitude to my mother, who had done a saintly job of accommodating her and taking care of her every need, she said to her son: 'I don't know why you married her . . . You always went for such glamour girls. Why don't you come back with me, Bob?'

'Mother, you don't understand,' my father instantly replied. 'There is no other woman for me, I worship the ground she walks on.'

I can report this verbatim because my mother, standing in the hallway, overheard every word and related it to her daughters. Not, I believe, to illustrate the character of Louise, but to reiterate the words that had nailed my father's colours to the mast.

And so our grandmother left, and inside our home the weather improved. But years later, despite her scorn, she asked to return. That was the first surprise. The second was that our remarkable mother agreed. I was in London in 1975 but Geraldine, studying at University of Sydney and still living at home, was left to suffer Louise's intrusion and complaints and my mother was left to care for her. When she died, it was Gloria who Louise wanted at her deathbed, holding her hand.

My father, always ready to wade in when witnessing an injustice, was completely silent when it came to discussing his mother's shortcomings. Not once in my life did I hear him utter a single negative word about the woman who, when he was aged five, had walked away from her tiny son, despite his begging her to stay. Only once did he reveal his broken but heroically forgiving heart. In a letter to Miki he wrote: '*My mother didn't let me have the life with her that I wanted.*'

Chapter Fourteen

I N JUST A LITTLE OVER six years of my father fixing peeling plaster, ancient plumbing or a leaky roof, and my mother cleaning and rearranging rented rooms, they had saved enough to sell the improved terraces and buy, outright, free and clear, a brick Federation house further out west in Concord. It was a time of huge happiness and satisfaction for them both.

Days and nights had been quiet at our house in Ashfield, but when we moved to Concord at the end of 1960, they barely whispered. Workdays were stamped with a regular pattern— sleep, rise for office/school/housework, sleep. Weekends were strictly somnolent.

My father, in 1961, had reached the age of fifty-four. He was working as a proof-reader at the *Australian Women's Weekly* and still performing: rarely on TV (younger faces were preferred), sometimes at clubs, but by 1963 mainly on radio, on shows like ABC's *Streamline*. He worked on arrangements, occasionally gave lessons to young singers he believed had talent, and he taped, as he had in the past, vocals for composers trying to attract recording contracts or opportunities for broadcasting. When not making one of these decreasing forays into the wider world, he would bounce along in shorts, knee-high socks, short-sleeved wash-and-wear shirts, hand-knitted vests and sensible rubber-soled shoes. My mother kept pace in her plain housedresses. Once or twice, the accoutrements of her old world mistakenly tumbled from the depths of her wardrobe: a frilled and pearl-studded pair of suede gloves; a velvet muff; a sequinned collar; a silver-linked belt. It was as if an Egyptian tomb had been unearthed. As I draped myself in these wonders, I marvelled at the glittering world in which my mother had once travelled.

Our parents rarely ventured out and entertaining at home was infrequent. Neighbours would drop in for tea and my mother's legendary scones (smothered in butter, jam and huge dollops of cream). There was open house on Christmas Eve (complete with sherry and ham and Christmas cake on the sideboard), plus occasional lunches for extended family (always punctuated by singing Irish songs), and canasta nights with musician friends— my sister recalls the popular entertainers, Enzo and Peggy Toppano, among them, but I can only remember being rocked to sleep by their laughter. But, most evenings, my parents' muffled voices drifting down the hall would be the last thing I'd hear. Either they'd be murmuring about the book they were reading or finishing off my mother's daily habit of completing the cryptic crossword, batting back ideas on the letters needed for down or across.

The mingling scent of my mother's lipstick, her face powder and a perfume called Tweed, were the signal that we were about to escape the suburbs and even now, should the air conjure it, this heady mixture would cause me undue excitement. But I could count on my hands how many outings we had per year. As for holidays, throughout my entire childhood and adolescence, they could be counted on one.

While we grew up never wanting for necessities, money was tight. There were instances (the cost of braces for our teeth, for example) that made us anxiously aware any extra, unplanned expenses were major obstacles in balancing our parents' meagre finances. We never had a car, but there were other reasons, apart from the money. Citing the car crash my father had had some twenty years before in America, my mother worried about his drinking and driving, and she had no wish to learn how to drive herself.

Sundays began with the boredom of saving my immortal soul. Mass on any day was long, but on Sundays it seemed eternal. The extra trail of parishioners shuffling up for communion didn't help, but it was the fact that the parish priest felt obliged to bore for twenty-five minutes, delivering sermons whose darkness and dreariness were equalled only by the architecture in which we sat. Perhaps the better educated and more skilful orators had been posted to more salubrious suburbs, in the belief that those with money needed that extra oomph to push them through the eye of the needle. The only riveting sermons I heard were made by Jesuits, sent out like missionaries to secondary schools to instruct convent girls that, should they find themselves in close proximity to the opposite sex, the devil lurked in every detail. They conjured an inferno to rival Dante's and had the immediate effect of sending those classmates indulging in the very closest of proximity to boys, rushing to confession. A few weeks later, when these girls stopped taking communion, it signalled that fear had dissipated and they were dodging God's bullets once again.

After the tedious Sunday hour at church, my survival prize was a visit to the local milk bar on the bleak corner of Parramatta and Burwood Roads, where my school friend and I would break our communion fast. There we'd sit in a tomb of green Formica, drinking our chocolate milkshakes, looking like the brides of Superman in blue capes to mid-calf and white net frothing out from the top of our heads—our Children of Mary outfits. Then I'd drag myself home down the dull asphalt street and await the ritual that made me a true believer, the baked dinner.

Nothing else my mother ever cooked equalled it. When I left home, there wasn't an enormous amount on our mother's culinary calendar that I missed. Certainly not the thick shoe-leather lamb's fry. And not the sausages, boiled pale grey and slimy, and then casseroled in Keen's Curry Powder—creating a dish as far removed from India as Antarctica. Garlic was used only when we had spaghetti Bolognese, and any lingering effect of that small single clove was followed up the next morning with a chlorophyll tablet before we were allowed out into the world.

But our mother's baked dinners were a wonder and, try as my sister and I might in our later lives in our kitchens on the opposite sides of the world, we could never replicate them. We finally figured it came down to the yellow tin sitting faithfully in the back of the fridge that was labelled *Dripping*. This little container was an archaeological dig, holding layer upon layer of flavours from various Sundays past—Proust could always find a madeleine, but our mother's dripping was unrepeatable. We named it the 'family retainer'.

After lunch, Sundays completely flat-lined. My five-year old sister had the swing and the garden to poke around in (and later her chemistry set on the back veranda). I, at twelve years of age, had the pogo stick, yo-yo, hula-hoop, or the front veranda for entertainment. Either I'd have jumping competitions with my Children of Mary friend, leaping off the metre high porch over the rhododendrons onto the lawn, or, as a last resort to beat off boredom, Geraldine and I would sit on the porch and play 'My car, your car', a feeble entertainment where the only hope was that a Ferrari would speed by when your turn came around, instead of a clapped-out Holden ute. But as a luxury sports car roaring down Burwood Road, Concord, was as likely as the Popemobile, the game offered little excitement. Meanwhile the soundtrack to our slo-mo Sundays could have been any of the following: the radio tuned to a cricket match, the drone of a lawnmower (but, more likely, the starter motor refusing to start), the clanking pedal on the Singer sewing machine (but, more likely, the bobbin spinning out of control), the rustle of newspaper or library book pages, the clicking of my mother's knitting needles flashing through some fabulously complicated pattern, or my father's pen scrawling in white heat across a writing pad.

As I grew older, I'd escape those sleepy suburban Sundays by catching a bus and then a train to the city and the golden triangle of the Domain—to look at the paintings in the Art Gallery of New South Wales, or at the books in the State Library, or to listen to the Sunday speakers in the park, that happy band of brothers (there were never any women) interesting enough to be labelled 'Ratbags', who would be either raving or cajoling from their soapboxes, insisting mankind could be saved—usually from the devil or politicians.

While there was definitely enough political discussion at home to keep me satisfied, in the limbo of my mid-teens I considered my parents among the last on the planet to understand how it turned—particularly as my father wouldn't countenance listening to my hero's comments on world order because he believed Bob Dylan sounded like 'a constipated manic howling over the asylum wall'. However, I was always aware that a 'fair go' was their ethic, the underdog their cause, and the preservation of Sydney and the country their hope. My mother made the political personal with those who came within her radius. When our white bread suburb of Concord was leavened with an influx of Greek and Turkish immigrants, she was constantly helping those who hadn't perfected their English by filling out forms and explaining how to leap across bureaucratic divides. Thank-you notes in the form of dolmades, baklava and other Mediterranean delights rattled the walls of our kitchen.

—

IN A RARE MOMENT in the last year of my teens, when I found time to concentrate on someone other than myself, I resolved to bring romance back into my parents' marriage. If anyone could do it, I believed Claude Lelouch had a chance. He was the French writer and director of the most romantic movie I had ever seen, *A Man and a Woman*.

La da da dadadada da . . . la da da dadadada da . . . went its theme music as the windscreen wipers caught the rain outside the lovers' car and the electricity sparking within. On the verge of turning twenty, I dreamed of a man who, at the end of dinner, would reply to the waiter's question 'Will there be anything else?' with 'Yes, coffee and a room.' Not that I, struggling to remain a good Catholic virgin, had any of the qualifications required to be sitting opposite such a sophisticate.

I purchased tickets to this movie for their twentieth wedding anniversary gift, and promised them dinner on their return. I obviously lived in a fool's dream because not knowing how to cook peas I decided to serve duck *à l'orange*. I spent most of my week's wages at David Jones Food Hall and, while I trusted Lelouch was sprinkling my parents with fairy dust, with the help of my sweet and obliging eleven-year-old sister, amid much laughter and angst, the recipe was pondered and by some miracle resolved.

The duck was a success, but not so the movie. 'Yes, lovely darling,' they murmured dismissively and, despite my endless prompting, that was all they would allow. It was a let-down, because on their return I'd half-expected my father to be renewed to the extent that he would have carried my starry-eyed mother over the threshold. Of course I had been mistaken on two counts: one, my parents' marriage required no shot to the arm; and, two, they saw the film for what it was, simply a delicious piece of confectionery.

Nineteen years before, my father had written to his bride: '*Honi ba wa wiki wiki nui nui loa*—on the occasion of our first wedded year.' Loosely translated, his declaration was an assurance to my mother that, although the year had gone quickly, his love was very, very long.

Across the years he would write of her as '*his darling . . . his one true love . . . the most wonderful, the most restrictive, the most respected woman I ever met*'. He used the word 'restrictive' in the sense that she discouraged alcohol in the house (exceptions being the odd bottle of Resch's beer in the fridge, a dusty bottle of sherry, and her Christmas cake, into which she poured rum with wild abandon). My father was always effusive with his words of love and, if those words had transmogrified into jewels, my mother would have possessed a glittering trunk full of them. As it was, I don't ever remember him unexpectedly bringing home a bunch of flowers or a box of chocolates: 'Red Tulip' or 'Winning Post' were reserved for the cinema. On her birthday and at Christmas, all I recall him presenting was a steam and dry iron or a pair of slippers (not the feathery Monroe kind, more the Andy Capp tartan style) and it seemed to me that he kept these two items in constant rotation. Thought was not something my father put into his rare forays into gift giving (although he had written an inscription into my *Alice in Wonderland*, I knew it had been purchased by my mother).

Around about our fortieth Christmas together, my sister and I finally admitted to each other to have grown tired of his Christmas Eve purloining of our wrapping paper. But, as our father always knew where things 'should be kept' in our mother's haphazard house, and could successfully direct us to sticky-tape and scissors, we continued to accept this as a quid pro quo. He never let money run away from him unless it galloped towards the bookie or the barmaid. As a child he collected coins, once remarking that the hobby 'thrilled him to his toes'.

But what he lacked in the bestowing of the material he more than made up for in physical affection. Returning home each night, if unmolested by alcohol, he would seek out my mother and greet her as though they had been parted for a year. My sister and I would always be motioned into the midst of the bear-like embrace—making us, my father would say, 'the ham in the sandwich'.

I would join delightedly in this ritual, but for some inexplicable reason I could never be the instigator of a kiss or a cuddle. Revealing my emotions was a problem. For example, despite a smorgasbord of punishments meted out to me from the age of five—Sister Elizabeth favoured the cane, three on one hand, three on the other, while Sister Bridget preferred three rulers on top of each other and delivered onto the knuckles—it wasn't until I was ten that I cried in public.

On this day, we had all been instructed to concentrate on our lesson, but instead I'd devoted all my attention to watching the wind playing with the silver-leafed tree just outside our classroom window. Mrs Douglas, a lay teacher at the convent, caned me so energetically that she produced a dark bruising of convict-like stripes on my legs; but what made me cry was the fact that, every time she asked me a question relating to the algebraic equation on the blackboard, I had to reply pathetically, 'I don't know.'

'I don't know,' whack. 'I don't know,' whack. The humiliation went on so long it eventually brought tears, and from the tears came the real pain—exposure: my crumpled face was on full show as I walked back through the classroom to my desk. Such a display never happened again. In my final school year, Sister Maureen memorably wrote on my report card: 'Darleen takes punishment so well I can't help but oblige her by giving more.'

In a letter to her father, Miki once said: *'There just isn't enough hugging in this world.'* Reading those words years later stung me, for I recalled that, as I grew up, my father had never received anywhere near enough hugs from me. He craved affection and it is only now, by threading together his early years, I realise it makes perfect sense. He had been, he wrote to Miki, 'reborn' when Geraldine, his 'late in life surprise', arrived in 1955. Bringing her home from the hospital, long before safety belts, she had gone to sleep on his shoulder and his 'world was made'.

Not only had I been a difficult baby, but my mother was nervous and overly protective whenever my father tried to get involved in my care. Geraldine, on the other hand, was a joy, an easy baby full of smiles; and, with my mother more relaxed, my father's role became far more balanced. I would watch the delight on his face when Geraldine ran to him with open arms and nestled in his lap, demonstrating all the love I longed to show. I remember wanting so badly to follow my little sister's lead but it was as if Medusa had cast her spell and I would stand, riveted to the spot, frozen by some kind of mysterious embarrassment. And then, just as mysteriously, in the last few years at home I changed my unfathomable ways and hugs and kisses were easily dispensed.

Chapter Fifteen

'HOW DO YOU DO,' my sister Geraldine greeted the stranger at the door. Then she swiftly followed that formality with a pressing question: 'Have you got a lolly?'

She was just two months shy of her second birthday, at the stage when most infants are mastering just a few words. But she chatted on in sentences and, in the manner of the fine journalist she would become, reported the who and the what and the wherefore, even throwing in a weather report as she climbed up on a stool by the window and declared: 'Darleen's went to see television . . . it's not raining anymore.'

This precocity, reported in a newspaper article, was the first sign that words would flow from my sister. She would begin as a cadet journalist covering the greyhound races; move onto Australian environmental issues; then to business reporting in the USA; become a war correspondent in the Middle East; write an award-winning memoir, then a world-wide bestselling novel, and then another. Until one afternoon her kitchen phone rang with unexpected news. After that, her phone would continue to jangle well into the night. When the doorbell rang, she was on yet another phone call and so her young son, Nathaniel, raced to open the front door. Anxious to share the news that was causing his parents so much excitement, he shouted out to the flower deliveryman: 'My mother just got a Pulitzer Surprise!'

Our mother would have been filled with joy at the news of such a prestigious award but, by 2005, she had withdrawn from the world to such an extent that it seemed the most glittering prize she could be offered was to name the faces of the people she loved. Our father, had he lived, would have puffed up to the size of a Michelin man in his pride at such an achievement by his 'little wizard with words', who had more than lived out his dreams.

Our father had written all his life. As we grew up, we would find him, on weekends and often late on weeknights, at the kitchen table hunched over a pad or aerogram, deep in concentration, scribing his thoughts as cigarette smoke swirled above his head like thought bubbles.

He had qualified for the University of California after graduating high school, but there was no family money available for college. California's steady beat of boom and bust had been visited upon the Conkeys. The move to Fullerton did nothing for the family fortune. The paint store proved a failure and all investment was lost. As always, John's work ethic prevailed and, despite pushing seventy, he was back in business, raising his 'Attorney at Law' shingle once again.

Meanwhile his grandson's dream of becoming a fulltime journalist came to nought. For a short period Robert won a part-time position, as general reporter on the *Fullerton Tribune*; yet, despite his pieces having been published in the local papers while he was still at high school and having filed news stories for the *LA Times* and the *LA Examiner*, there was no hope of permanency anywhere. So, to make regular money, he was forced to take a twelve-hour-a-day job in a steel mill, carrying patterns to the casting department. Later, at the age of twenty, while working for twelve dollars a week as a vegetable store hand, 7 a.m. to 7 p.m., seven days a week with one Sunday off per month, he followed his dream to be a 'serious' writer, scribing away under the counter when he could find the time.

He received a confetti fall of rejection slips. One of the few considered responses during that period was a letter from Burton Roscoe, editor of *Bookman* in New York City, who wrote in reply to one of his hopeful profile pieces: '*Unfortunately your appreciation of Dr Corby seems more of a rave than a more balanced consideration of his merits.*'

He came close to writing the biography of the novelist, Joseph Hergesheimer, but he lacked the cash to get him east to Pennsylvania to interview the man.

All the while he wrote across the board—some poetry, as well as short stories for popular magazines.

Just one month off turning twenty-one, he got a break. Above a photograph of a young man clad in the writer's garb of cardigan and corduroy pants, the headline in the Santa Ana newspaper read: '*Robert Cutter, Fullerton writer . . . has just disposed of two stories to a magazine. He plans to make writing his life work.'* Street and Smith, the publishers of *Sports Story*, paid him a cent a word and, with a string of stories running to many thousands of words, he made good money. He had followed the golden rule and written about what he knew. It showed in his writing, where imaginative drama married seamlessly to the technical aspects of baseball and gridiron.

Despite Al Jolson luring him into singing and away from this first career, throughout his life he wrote. In Honolulu, he wrote radio shows. On the road, he wrote songs. While laid up in an army hospital in New Guinea, he wrote a short story published by the Australian monthly, *Man* (the *Playboy* of its era). Back in Sydney for seven years, he wrote a regular column for *Music Maker*. Across the years, he wrote odes to the city of Sydney and entered a competition to write an anthem for Australia. He wrote songs to his daughters and his wife. He wrote elegies for his heroes. He wrote short stories and plays involving murder and multifarious misdemeanours. He wrote about the meaning of life and the price of bread to his American daughter. Later, when his Australian daughters became ex-pats, he wrote to them both, keeping them up to date with home life and all things Aussie.

And he wrote hundreds of letters, across four decades, to governments, business leaders, politicians and editors, offering his views, both extolling and criticising, on anything and everything: education and teachers' strikes, freedom of disclosure on police corruption, unions, cuts to the ABC, the establishment of the TAB, the annexation of the Golan Heights, Iran, interest rates, nuclear versus hydro power, the misuse of the English language, the game of cricket, the sport of kings, the damming of the Franklin. He wrote a thesis on how the Labor Party could win the next election and, after he was taken on as an assistant proof-reader, he immediately wrote to the newspaper's proprietor with advice on how he might bolster sales.

He was universal in his outreach. Instead of leaving his usual annual thank you to the garbage collectors in the form of money or beer, one Christmas he left this:

If you are the garbos we've had all year
You all should be pissed off without a tear
You've waked us, you've shaked us, until we get wild
And now you expect us to give like Rothschild
Well, boyos, we've got news no fear
Give us a quiet good job all through the year
Then we'll unbutton the fridge or the purse
If not, dear boyos, you'll get the reverse.

Fiercely opinionated, but always well informed, he lined his facts up like soldiers, used interesting and intricate sentences that were always perfectly punctuated and grammatically correct.

Even before he uttered his first 'I do', he was faithfully wedded to the English language, and throughout his life he adored and defended it. His love letters poured from the tea chest under such titles as '*Gobbledygook? Or Correct Communication?*' and '*Our English Language. Respect It*' and '*Why Are We Denigrating Our English Language?*' When he spotted abuse of the rules of grammar, a letter would be fired off to offending editors, and apologies would be forthcoming. I give one example from among many of such dispatches: '*We have this physical impossibility of what has become the peripatetic centre. Centre around, centres around—what a ludicrous picture this conjures up. A centre can only be surrounded, it can surround nothing, yet even notable physicists have been guilty of this totally erroneous usage.*'

I draw a curtain across his thoughts on punctuation for, as he admits and then sets about to prove, it is 'a subject that could occupy a small thesis'.

My father spread his political net wide. I found a note from the Ministry of Defence in the State of Israel; a thoughtful reply from the Chairman of the Council of Economic Advisers in Washington, complete with research attached; correspondence from Premier Wran and various MPs, Jim and Allan Fraser and Jim Cairns among them; a two-page letter from Malcolm Fraser's office defending the proposed hydro-electric development in Tasmania, to which the entire family was vehemently opposed; a note from Robert Menzies; a telegram from Gough Whitlam thanking him for his 'suggestions and support'; and a personal letter from Bob Hawke, discussing nuclear power and enquiring after my father's health. There was his elegy to King George, and an ode to Churchill that received a letter of thanks from the Queen and praise from the *Australian Women's Weekly*.

While Lawrie Brooks was an honest writer, some on the receiving end may have welcomed a little more restraint in opinion and a little less gusto in verbiage: in 1946, the editor of *Australian Digest* declined my father's essay supporting a

Jewish State, declaring it 'explosive cargo'. In 1974, prominent publisher and bookseller, Max Harris, replied to heaven knows what was vexing my father: *'Thank you for your comments—despite their deflationary effect.'* In 1975, the besieged MP for Moreton and former minister, Jim Killen, responded: *'I have read with interest the views you have so vigorously expressed.'*

Among this varied lot, I hauled out a bunch of yellowed newspaper clippings of his 'Letters to the Editor'. These letters were published in every Sydney newspaper to the extent that, when they became too numerous, rather than flood the market, he used his original surname of Cutter.

As I read through these letters, my father entered the room, standing square on with shoulders back and tummy in, perfectly balanced on the balls of his feet, like a lightweight boxer readying himself for a counterpunch. And I heard him again, projecting his perfectly enunciated words (a tense clipped tone and volume set on high if he'd been drinking).

He could be irritatingly bellicose while standing his ground for any idea or ideal he believed in. In his lexicon, Israel could do no wrong; he was unabashedly pro the unions and pro Labor; and, if you happened to be having a go at George Moore or Donald Bradman, kings of his chosen sports, he would defend them to the death.

———

WHILE OUR FATHER DISCIPLINED the language, our mother played with it. In her late twenties, she wrote a weekly column for the *ABC Weekly* titled 'Studio News & Views'. Then, after a hiatus of some thirty years, she found the time, inclination and confidence to begin writing again, and her wry and humorous pieces began appearing regularly in the *Sydney Morning Herald*.

A letter she wrote during those years illustrates her wonderful slanted view of the world. I can see her now, sitting down at the old ink-stained oak dining table with a cup of tea by her side and writing this to her family living at the opposite side of the globe, to amuse and to remind them of home:

Dear Mrs Possum,

I hope you do not mind me writing to you, after all we have never met, but as we are dual tenants, and have been for eleven years, I'm sure you'll take this letter in a spirit of friendship as it is meant.

It is hard to know exactly where you reside in this house—perhaps under it—but nightly I hear your family making merry in the wall cavities, so I guess you spread around some.

I had the pleasure of meeting, well not exactly meeting, you understand, but bumping into your husband several years ago when he called in the side door one night and made merry with my hanging lightshade in the spare bedroom. It looked like fun and sounded great, the chains squeaking like an old swing. Our Kelpie, 'George', was so interested he went into a trance till I locked him in the bathroom. Your husband, Mrs Possum, is not a little creature, never have I seen such thighs, but his personality seems fun-loving, which must be a comfort to you if you spend much time on the damp ground under this house. I must add that he appeared physically fit and I am pleased that the covers on the twin beds were nylon (not usually appreciated by me but bequeathed by an aged mother) and so could be taken out of the room and soaked and scalded without damage.

We almost met last year when I opened my window seat and became quite overcome to see that a 'happy event' had taken place in it. I'm glad you, or one of your daughters, had a warm confinement amid my best blankets and hope the effort of scratching holes in the middle of them didn't tire the little mother. I was sorry, however, that you had no real confetti for the rather late wedding and had to make your own with some newspaper cuttings I was keeping to remind me of the beginning of my daughter's journalistic career, and my eldest daughter's wedding.

We now have duvets to keep us warm these days so don't worry about the blankets, which are no more, and I've seen the babes in the gum trees and they are cute with their bright eyes and pink noses, well worth it I'd say. You must be proud.

The reason for this letter is to ask a favour. Do you have any influence with your husband and young sons? I hear them crashing across the tin roof of our abode at four o'clock each afternoon. No worries! I'm usually preparing vegetables or reading at that time so that's no problem—though I've seen strong visitors go pale and slop their afternoon teas on the first onslaught. No, I am not complaining, let me assure you. No doubt your ancestors were on this spot long before 1921 when this house was capped by aluminium roof and intrusive chimney posts, so you, in all justice, have the prior claim. However the 4 a.m. return is something else. Do you think you could induce your mate and offspring to tippy-toe or at least not crash as if from a great height? I'm sure it's just a sign that tummies are full and hearts are ditto with joie d' vivre, and I've had a similar experience with my own husband many a time, but have finally semi-trained him to enter quietly after his nights out.

The problem is I'm starting to adopt Possum schedules, sleeping most of the day and awake all night. My eyes and nose are undoubtedly turning pink and thighs thickening. I'm worried and hope you can help remedy the situation.

I'm slipping this letter down the back of the fireplace, which I know you frequent. It's not likely I'll get a reply back as it would be fanciful to think you could write but I know you are an avid reader by the way you devoured my daughter's articles.

Sincerely yours, but tired,

Gloria Brooks

P.S. My husband and son-in-laws would like to know what it is your husband chews and does it grow around here?

Chapter Sixteen

AccORDING TO THE CATHOLIC CHURCH, if a kiss was 'passionate', and you were unmarried and indulging in such displays of affection, it was a mortal sin and you could kiss your immortal soul goodbye. In my late teens, I found the tipping point difficult to gauge, but eventually supposed that if a kiss felt like Heaven, then Hell was close behind. Reluctant to face an eternity of punishment, I was a constant penitent at St Patrick's church, situated conveniently close to where I worked in the city. In fact, I became such a regular customer that, in December 1967, noting down the name of the priest above the confessional door, I sent him a Christmas card.

My parents' wish was that I wouldn't leave home until I was married and, although I longed for more freedom, it didn't cross my mind to disobey. I definitely dragged my feet in the growing-up department. My father confirmed this in a letter to Miki when I was aged nineteen: *'Darleen is a slow maturer ranging in manifestation from a twelve-year-old to a seemingly sophisticated late twenties.'* But, by the age of twenty, the laws of nature, church and state combined to make me grow up fast. In a one-off event with my non-Catholic boyfriend, one that seemed over before it began, I became pregnant. I couldn't tell my parents. Although many years later my sister would be my first female confidante, at this point I told no one.

Now that I know my father's history, I realise I could have told him anything. Certainly, my mother would have been my sanctuary. But I couldn't bear seeing their faces filled with shock, worry and disappointment, and so I saw doctors—one after another. Each one turned me away. I was just six months shy of controlling my own destiny. The law in 1968 required that any female under the age of twenty-one obtain her parents' consent and signature before her pregnancy could be terminated. At the time of writing in 2019, abortion in the state of New South Wales was still a criminal offence.

My local GP sent me to a Macquarie Street doctor, who then referred me to a GP in Potts Point. There, anxiously waiting my turn, I found myself sitting next to Chips Rafferty (strange now learning he was an old friend of my father's). Perhaps he guessed from my face the secret I had managed to hide from those closest to me for, as I passed him on my way into the doctor's surgery, from his great lanky height he gave me a salute and then bent down to whisper in his unmistakable accent, 'Good luck!'

But I was out of luck: no registered doctor could help me. Finally, one Saturday, knowing I might die but beyond reasoning what a far greater tragedy that would have been for my parents, I kept an appointment with an abortionist practising out of modern, accountant-like offices, in a building opposite the War Memorial in Elizabeth Street. A few young women sat in a waiting room, women who, like me, were grateful for the company and the empathetic faces of the female receptionist and nurse. The walls were crowded with photographs of racehorses and, as I sat counting down the minutes of my life, I was forced to listen to a conversation between my 'doctor' and his bookie that seemed to last an eternity. I registered under the name of a friend. Years later, I discovered that she too had resorted to using a different name at this same place, that very same year.

For months after, all I wanted to do was sleep. In my spare time, I sat and sketched weeping faces in pen and ink. And, in confined spaces, I suffered shortness of breath, walking out of the cinema and the theatre in the middle of shows. Finally, I hauled myself out of the darkness but not before returning to my first boyfriend, a good Catholic, confiding in him, and then marrying before the year was out.

It was shortly after this, when visiting my local priest, the age of reason finally kicked in. When I told him I wouldn't be able to receive communion because I was taking the Pill (the contraceptive pill had been available for less than eight years and only to married woman with a prescription), the priest waved my concern away. His explanation was that it was simply a matter of conscience. 'Fine for me,' I said, 'but what of the women living in countries like South America, or even Ireland—mothers anxious about being able to continue to feed the children they already had?' We both knew they would be excommunicated.

In protest, I excommunicated myself. It was a memorable morning the Sunday I stayed in bed waiting for lightning to strike, while my fervent Catholic husband went to Mass to pray for his wife who had lost her faith. Years later, after the divorce, came an annulment and the marriage was wiped clean off the Catholic slate.

Now a line in one of my father's letters makes me wonder if he, at around the same age, might have felt as marooned as I had been, unable to confide in his family.

When my sister Geraldine arrived home from her first stint in America, where she both studied and practised journalism, she brought with her a fellow student from Columbia, a handsome American journalist called Tony Horwitz, who had recently become her husband. Tony never forgot his initiation ceremony into my father's tell-it-like-it-is bluntness. On a bar stool at the corner pub, he learned that, shortly after his new father-in-law lost his virginity at the age of twenty-two, it wasn't to any rafter-ringing applause but to low murmurings from a doctor informing him he'd contracted a venereal disease. But despite my father's bent for laying bare the facts even when the listener had no wish to know, when he told this story he neglected crucial detail. The only word he allowed to describe the event that landed him in LA County General Hospital was 'dreadful'.

I tried guessing the circumstances of this major life experience. Had his father, Winnie, or his friend, Stanley Smith, felt it was more than time for him to be initiated into manhood and pointed him in the direction of the red-light district? Or had an older woman seduced him? Or had it been simply an encounter with an experienced woman of similar age? I could find no evidence to back any of these assumptions and so I was left asking why, in relation to this event, didn't my father complete the story. But then I found a possible answer, suggested in a letter to my sister—a few words I had missed on a first reading.

When Geraldine worked for the *Sydney Morning Herald*, she reported on the Franklin River campaign, the fight to save Australia's last wild river from a hydro-electric scheme. Many spoke out against the plan, but no voice was more powerful than that of a Tasmanian medical doctor by the name of Bob Brown. From 1976 through to the historic High Court judgment in favour of the Commonwealth against Tasmania in 1986, Brown ceaselessly defended the river—at one point spending almost three weeks in prison.

There was much to love and admire about Bob Brown, and my sister did. She covered the Franklin saga comprehensively, travelling with him on a couple of reporting trips into the southwest wilderness and out to the Splits of the Gordon River. While driving her back to Hobart airport after one of those treks, Brown, perceiving my sister's feelings for him, gently revealed that he'd known he was gay from a very young age. 'He very kindly warned me off,' she told me.

My father, learning of this, wrote to her and revealed something he had locked away for many decades:

I have certainly seen enough of the dedicated Dr Brown recently to understand your interest in him. My God, such sacrifice and dedication is almost unbelievable. With it is a rather lovable personality. So, he flirted with the homo bit—so what—your dad had a dab at the lot but finished up in his early 20's desiring only the most desirable of femmes.

Chapter Seventeen

AFTER COMPLETING A TYPING and shorthand course at the urging of my parents ('Something to fall back on,' they said) from Monday to Friday I was on the early train to the city making what was to be a two-year journey. It would take that long, and a couple of secretarial jobs, before I was paid not just to type but to write.

In my first secretarial job, I worked at Australian Consolidated Press. Occasionally, I would find myself riding up in the lift with Frank Packer, the man who owned and ran the company. I would cast furtive glances at the media giant—his imposing figure made taller still by the felt hat that in the 1960s was the required uniform of city gents—all the while hoping that he wouldn't turn his gaze towards me as I stood there hiding behind my Twiggy-style false eyelashes, a Jean Shrimpton-style deep fringe, and a curtain of hair that was longer than my skirt.

There was a story told at the time that was destined to become legend. The word was that Packer had recently fired a boy in the lift because he sported a Beatles cut—hair worn slightly above the eyes and skimming the ears. In the view of the old guard, these small extensions to the traditional short back and sides flaunted disregard for both decency and masculinity. It was a funny story because of the punchline: the bemused boy exiting the lift that day, clutching a week's wages shoved into his hand by Packer, was a messenger, and not on the mogul's payroll.

My memory of that time is clouded by cigarette smoke swirling in lifts, buses, trains, planes, restaurants, cinemas, theatres and offices, and an unlovely image shines clear through that fog—the myriad of cream-and-green tiled pubs, not unlike public lavatories, found on almost every corner of a city block, the odour of stale hops wafting out onto the street as the doors swung open. These were places devoted to 'men's business', sacrosanct temples worshipping beer on tap: a public place banned to women. On one occasion, exiled to the 'Ladies Lounge' in the pub next to the Consolidated Press building, I ordered what I believed to be an earth-shatteringly sophisticated brandy and dry. As I stood at the bar, the adjoining door to the Public Bar swung open, exposing a din of competing voices and a crush of men. At that moment I caught a glimpse of Lawrie Brooks.

My father and I worked in the same building. One unforgettable day he left his proof-reading pals and picked me up from the Circulation Department, where I spent my working week bored to the bone, and took me on a tour of the building to show me the power behind the press. I saw an entire floor devoted to storing paper, huge cylindrical shapes, standing in long lines like fat white tanks ready to roll into battle. And I visited the compositing floor, where boys, carrying screeds from Editorial, ran between the typesetters, who used their metal alphabet to create long galleys of words, and where the compositors, bent over trays of 'slugs', filled pages with those hot metallic words—words that when inked and pressed onto paper would spread the news of the day throughout the city. I had never seen anything more exciting in my life: the urgency of the labour, the promise of the presses rolling. The might of it thrilled me, but it was salt to the wound. I couldn't be a part of it.

———

EVENTUALLY, I FOUND JOBS in advertising agencies: the first as secretary in the Film Production Department and the second as PA to a Creative Director. All the time I would be pestering the senior creatives (Bryce Courtenay for one) by presenting cringe-worthy ideas, until finally the rejections taught me how to shape and tighten my writing to the point where it was print, film or radio ready. Shortly after I earned the title 'copywriter', I gained the prefix 'Mrs' and, a month before my twenty-first birthday, I began my Marriage That Never Was.

The creative departments where I worked—in Sydney, Melbourne, Los Angeles and London—brimmed with art directors and copywriters who, like me, dreamed of other lives as film directors, photographers, artists, writers, singers, composers. Ray Lawrence would follow me around the agency, clicking away, the camera lens constantly attached to his eye. Peter Carey would amble in on Mondays, offering perusal of short stories he'd written over the weekend. In Los Angeles, I worked with the composer of some of The Beach Boys' classic hits, and my creative director became a Hollywood screenwriter. In my London agency, where Salman Rushdie and Fay Weldon had previously warmed the seats, my art director was lead singer and composer of songs in a band. Years later, when I was walking in St James Square with the poet Peter Porter, past the building where I had worked, he told me that he too had once been a copywriter.

Describing how crunchy and fresh canned vegetables were, or rhapsodising over how a lipstick could turn the world into a rainbow wasn't fulfilling, but the company made up for it. We would lurk in each other's offices, slouch in door frames, or hang around the coffee machine, telling jokes, discussing the latest and the best until deadlines were upon us and fear of failure, with the accompanying adrenaline, sent us rushing towards typewriters and layout pads.

When I worked in the USA and the UK, I found myself in a box set of *Mad Men*. The most frequent order from management in Los Angeles was for 'a triple dry martini, straight up and hold the olive'; in London, around mid-morning, the order of the day was 'We shall convene this meeting at the Golden Lion', and it was sherry or champagne for elevenses. Expense account lunches rolled into expense account dinners. Breakfast meetings were unheard of because the majority of us were either sleeping it off, or sleeping with someone from the office.

While being a copywriter enabled me to travel the world, in my mind it was a runner-up career to being a Brenda Starr or

Lois Lane, girl reporter. But that was a dream built on another dream. The only subjects worth mentioning on my high school report cards were Art and English; but to matriculate I needed a pass in Maths, which was my nemesis. The nuns stymied my chance of applying for a scholarship into East Sydney National Art School, despite my flourishing in art class. In my final exams, I plummeted from top of the class to scraping a pass. When my mother queried this result, the nuns proudly told her that they had decided to mark me down because 'mixing with those bad types in the art world' would interfere with my pass mark into Heaven (not Holland, as I had once sincerely answered when the nun asked what word starting with H indicated a place we all wanted to go to). But, even if the major miracle of my passing Maths eventuated, my marks would have needed to be good enough to obtain a university scholarship: it would be another seven years before Gough Whitlam became Prime Minister and made tertiary education free. Yet I did know that, if I asked my parents to fund further schooling, they would have beggared themselves to do it (my sister saved them from this by winning a Commonwealth Scholarship for her final two years of schooling).

And so I said nothing, left school after the Intermediate Certificate, obtained my secretarial qualifications, and found myself on that city train. Every morning, as it stopped at Redfern Station, I longed to get off and join the crowd heading towards the University of Sydney. As compensation, I took night classes, one in Art and another in English, within the convict-hewn sandstone walls of the colonial Darlinghurst Gaol—a place of sad beginnings that had morphed into a place of hope. It was there, for the first time, I enjoyed informed and inspired teaching and learned how good it felt to see an A-plus against my name when the Leaving Certificate results were published. It would be another twenty-five years before I experienced that again, after gaining a BA with First Class English Honours and later when I completed a PhD.

My sister, Geraldine, kick-started the idea of my late-in-life study. Sitting together one morning, drinking coffee and shooting the breeze under a brilliantly blue New York City sky, we talked about regrets. I volunteered that, apart from a few men in my life, my only regret was missing out on university. 'Well, do it now,' my sister replied. 'There is nothing stopping you.' And she was right.

Unimpaired by the confusion of adolescence, the intensity of early adulthood, having raised my children, and forged a second career in London as a journalist and magazine editor, I was free to read and discuss. And having lived long enough to have been both the faithful and the faithless, the lover and the beloved, the betrayer and the betrayed, I discovered that I could be a fellow traveller of Captain Ahab and Mr Leopold Bloom and, on close acquaintance with Shakespeare's characters, I could recognise their delights and dilemmas. Had I stepped off that train at Redfern in my teenage years, those worlds and those people would have been beyond my scope.

My sister and I have influenced each other at many life-altering moments. After I moved to Melbourne for a copywriting job, Geraldine would come down and stay during her school holidays. She visited my advertising agency there; then later, in her university years while staying with me in London, she was entertained by many of the interesting folk in advertising who appeared to be having a party 24/7. When she returned to Sydney to continue at university, she began to talk seriously about dropping out, of forsaking her dream of a newspaper cadetship to work in the ad world.

I'd always believed, since she was a little girl, my sister would do something special with her life, so I did all I could to encourage her to continue with her study. In a letter from London I wrote to her:

Don't you think about leaving uni. You'd hate actually working. <u>WORKING</u>. Doesn't it make your blood run cold, kid? Getting up at 7.30–7.30! in the morning. Becoming a <u>weekender.</u> You're out of your little academic mind. You're almost there . . . come on now, in our old age I want a sister who can support me with a nice fat degree. How will we feed the cats, otherwise?

She gained her degree, won the cadetship, and within record time she was interrogating kings, queens, prime ministers, despots, captains of industry and becoming a Middle-Eastern war correspondent for the *Wall Street Journal*.

Now I think of my father in his twenties. No one for him to confide in, no one with shared experiences who knew him from the inside out, no one with such credentials that he could trust them unswervingly. If he had had this counsel and support, would his life have been different? Would he have steered clear of Rubey? Would he have kept his contract with Harry Owens, and with him become famous throughout the USA? Would he have stayed on in California and competed with his musical contemporaries? Would he have been encouraged to follow his dream and become a classical concert singer? But he had to find his path through life alone, while Ronald, the golden brother who left the world just as he arrived, always danced on ahead of him.

Then again, if any of those what-ifs had manifested, he never would have written this to my sister Geraldine:

You and Darleen, result of that gut-feeling marriage, consti-tute the height of success in my life. The fact, and fact it is, that I might have challenged Sinatra had I returned to the USA pales beside the joy you two have brought to Glor and me.

———

MY SISTER AND I share many traits, but the most obvious one to outsiders is our voice. Despite the decades of my living in England and Geraldine in America, little has changed in our accents and it is still difficult to tell our voices apart. I can't explain why. Perhaps it is the result of a blending of Australian and American. But I do remember how particular our parents were on correct pronunciation.

It wasn't to encourage any verbal posturing, I do know that, for I remember coming home from school one day and repeating to my father the lyrics to a song we had been taught,

'Carol Of The Birds'. Hearing my ridiculously plummy pronunciation of prancing 'par-ran-sing' and dancing 'darrn-sing', he
was horrified and instantly corrected my affectation. He had a
perfectly tuned ear for humbug.

Our singing voices are also, unfortunately, the same. When
we sing, we are mountain climbers in stilettos. But Joni Mitchell
is there, and her wonderful lyrics are there, and despite knowing
our expedition is doomed, time and again and across decades,
we attempt to ascend the heights. We have sung duets on rocky
tracks in Martha's Vineyard, trudging through the sand hills of
a Sydney beach, climbing ferny slopes of Wimbledon Common,
navigating the cobbles of a village in the Alpes-Maritimes,
in the shadow of the blue ridges of the Shenandoahs, and lost in
the hills on the outskirts of Florence. If Wilde was right, and
each man kills the thing he loves, then we have murdered
and murdered: 'Big Yellow Taxi', 'A Case Of You', 'River', 'Free
Man In Paris', 'The Last Time I Saw Richard', 'Carey', 'Both
Sides Now', and particularly 'California'.

I took lessons in piano, Geraldine in flute. The results were
dismal: musical DNA skipped us right on by. But if my father
was disappointed, he never showed it. All I remember is the
stifling of an amused curl to his lip when, at the age of seven,
after a special outing to the movies to watch David Niven circle
the globe in all forms of transport, I stood in front of his chair
and attempted to sing 'Around The World' for him.

By the time the curtain went up on my school choir seven
years later, and I saw my father's proud, optimistic face beaming
up at me in the school hall audience, I desperately fought off a

fit of giggles. I never had the heart to tell him I'd been rapidly demoted from soprano to alto, and finally to ignominy when I was instructed to 'just mouth the words'.

Being so well aware that to have a singing voice is to be blessed, I would like to know if my father ever sent a silent prayer of thanks to his great-grandfather, Ithamar, for passing down his musical talent. And when did the music begin? Perhaps Ithamar's forebears had voices of angels, too. Perhaps, among those colonists and revolutionaries, there were those who astonished their fellow brethren with songs that soared in the little wooden Massachusetts churches they helped build. All lost to the high thin air now.

But, then again, not all lost. One of his granddaughters is a professional cellist, one grandson plays the harp, and my son sits down at a piano or picks up a guitar and plays by sight and by ear. And he can sing.

Chapter Eighteen

I WAS WORKING IN an ad agency in Los Angeles at the time my father was declared an alien. I was responsible for opening the bureaucratic floodgates. Before I left for the States he had contacted the American Embassy to ask whether I had a right to an American passport. This alerted the US authorities to the whereabouts of their straying son and prompted the Australian Government to enquire how an American had been voting in elections and receiving an Australian pension for so many years.

He had slipped under the radar in 1941, while America was still debating whether to become involved in the Second World War. Impatient with his country's lack of resolve, my father told a white lie about his nationality so he could join in the fight against Hitler. By adopting his father's Canadian birthplace, this allowed him to join the 2nd AIF as a member of the British Commonwealth. During his four years in the army—in the heat and mud—he'd been recast as an Aussie to his AIF bootstraps.

He hadn't given his American citizenship any thought since then. But, once questions were asked, he immediately applied for Australian naturalisation. Shortly after, two tall men arrived unannounced on his Concord doorstep, sporting buzz cuts with an attitude that belied the 'secret' of their 'service'. When they walked down our hallway they passed a portrait in oil of Ithamar Conkey, looking completely out of time and place in Sydney's suburbia. He loomed there as a reminder that our father's ancestors were among the first American colonists. The buzz cuts sat at my parents' dining room table for hours, quizzing my father about name changes and dates; but, ultimately, trying to understand why he would possibly want to renounce his American citizenship and a heritage that, apart from the blip of his grandfather crossing the border to Canada, had begun over a century before teatime in Boston harbour, with both sides of the family fighting in the Revolutionary War and for the Union in the Civil War.

Perhaps he told them a little of what he wrote to his daughters. To Geraldine:

> You've apparently become accustomed to the New York pace because that's what Darleen's is, except that it is exercised in true British good taste—despite her underlying sense of true rough Aussie humour. Hope she never forgets she was born an Aussie, when Aussies were true Aussies, not the one-eye-on-the-dollar, the other on the next spinner-of-that-dollar idea to come out of the USA. I was so proud of being allied to this country and its people. It took me

six years to make me see the uniquely rugged, inven-
tive, clear-seeing, genuinely fit and active breed, the like
of which I had never seen before. In the big war it was
amazing. My Yank brothers were lost without their tools,
their mobile kitchens and fresh food supplies We Aussies
made do, we extemporised. The only way to stop those
Aussies doing something progressive was to bury them in
a block of cement. Even in my combat-harmless unit we
were never at a loss for long when shortages, unsuitable
terrain, mechanical trouble with vehicles, lack of shower
facilities, whatever, the problem was soon solved. I'm only
sorry I wasn't born an Aussie ... I truly hope that in the
outback and in some pockets of this formerly totally indi-
vidualistic country there still lives the spirit and resource
I saw in those early years.

When he first entered Australia, he had his linguistic ear
to the ground, writing that he had landed at 'Pier Eyeteen'.
A stranger on a strange shore, he couldn't have imagined that
Sydney would become his city for life. Thirty-five years later he
wrote to Miki:

You can visualise the slumberous City of Sydney I knew in
my first 15 years before the State and City Fathers awoke
to the fact that Sydney is not in any earthquake belt and
made the sky the limit. As is the way of avaricious 'devel-
opers' they've overdone it and without much thought
for architectural beauty or harmonizing of surrounds.

Nevertheless, this staunch lover of San Francisco as 'the greatest,' long before world opinion put it up high, is sold on his Sydney as the most exciting, cosmopolitan, somewhat uniquely almost beautiful, but definitely to me 'greatest' of them all. I really feel that I belong to Sydney and Sydney belongs to me—I am part of it.

In a song he composed about Sydney he wrote: '*The old world has its flair, but this town has an air, of city face and country grace ...*' And in an ode to the city he wrote: '*... that sweet shimmering majesty of harbour ... the unforgettable reason for your being ...*'

If this wasn't enough to inform the fellas from the American Embassy that he had become a dedicated Aussie, he might just have added the death blow, telling them as he had in a letter to Miki that, although he had once had a passion for baseball, cricket now surpassed it as '*the most fascinating bat and ball game of them all ... the chess game of active sport, a game of skill and imagination, relying very little on luck.*'

Declaring his love for Australia my father once quoted in a letter to Miki: '*Although I spent only half my life in it, strangely this is the place where I get ... "Breathes there the man with soul so dead, Who never to himself hath said, This is my own, my native land!"*'

I wonder if the Mayor who presided over the naturalisation ceremony in a hall in Concord Council Chambers in 1975 would have been familiar with those words of Sir Walter Scott. Certainly the majority in the hall didn't recognise much of what the Mayor had to say, as he addressed, as he put it, the 'New Australians', with patronising questions at a paralysing pace: 'Wh-airr ... dooo ... yooo ... livvee? ... Oh, by the traffic lights, nice spot!'

My father sat among the other migrants, though he was not quite so 'new', having lived in the country for over thirty-five years. After the ceremony, the Mayor, enormously put out by my mother and sister failing to quell their body-racking giggles, made a beeline for them, demanding to know what had caused so much hilarity. Geraldine managed to mumble something about our beer-hoisting, cricket-loving, army veteran father being an old hand at being Australian, and then fled.

——

DESPITE BEING HEAVILY OVERSHADOWED by his British son-in-law's 1.91-metre frame, my father basked in the company of Michael Bungey, the father of my two children and the reason I spent a quarter of a century away from my homeland. Whenever they were together, in London or Sydney, they played golf, went to pubs together, and talked and watched cricket, at the Sydney Cricket Ground and Lord's. The last conversation they had was discussing the scores of the 1994 Test Series at the SCG. My father revelled in the male company denied him by living in a house full of women: 'Everyone female, including the cat and dog ...' he'd complain.

I have always believed my father would have been happier if I'd been born a boy. He might then have filled in the great swathes of emptiness he experienced waiting, waiting, waiting for the company of his absent father. He took me to sports venues, but the games with their arcane rules were lost on me. Once I remember making him laugh through his disappointment at my lack of interest when, at a cricket match, I mistook the umpire for a player and asked for his autograph. He laid out sports board games for me to play, but they didn't hold my attention.

He closely followed my athletics at school and, when he proudly applauded my leading the winning relay team, I kept it from him that my speed was so slow I'd been relegated to the team in the year below. I made him happy when we played catch by successfully following his instruction to keep my eye on the ball. And when he came home and reported to my mother with excitement that my tennis coach considered I might have had the right stuff to be a serious player if I hadn't broken my wrist, I felt he harboured the vague hope that at least I could have been a contender. Of course, his Olympic-class father Winnie had made athletics an impossible act to follow. But that didn't stop my father as a young man from trying, despite Winnie not being there to coach him or to cheer him on.

Back in Fullerton, his friend Stanley went a good way to filling the yawning gap of his distant father. As did the captain of the football team at Fullerton High School, Ted Shipley, who was a star athlete (later, playing for Stanford University, he would score a touchdown in the Rose Bowl against Notre Dame). In Santa Maria, try as he might, my father had been a failure at sports and it amazed him when Shipley, someone he hero-worshipped, took a kindly interest in him.

He began bulking up, each morning packing into his slender frame six buckwheat pancakes drowned with butter and maple syrup, followed by three eggs and oatmeal porridge. It turned out to be the breakfast of champions and his '110-pound flyweight team' winning the High School Orange County Championship. It's a safe bet that the player having his picture taken with the team for the year book, standing in the back row trying to tame the growing smile on his face, with his slight shoulders held proudly back, is thinking about his father and hoping that he might now believe the moniker 'Buster' no longer applied.

The son attempting to seek his father's approval then turned to writing. In the article announcing his contract with Street and Smith, the newspaper reported: 'Young Cutter is following in the footsteps of his father, who has been sporting editor of a Sacramento daily for many years.' And it wasn't hard to detect the inspiration for the protagonist in his magazine story titled *The Runt*, a tale about a footballer called Buddy Foster, who in his first training game scored a touchdown from one end of the field to the other. For 'Runt' read undersized and undervalued, and then think 'Buster'.

In his late twenties, my father surprised himself when he played softball with a relatively talented group and discovered he was the best player of the day, being an excellent shortstop and batsman. Which raises the question: why did Winnie never encourage his son? His son never failed to see his father as a hero, but Winnie never acted like one. A published poem written by Winnie—an elegy to an energetic little boy with golden hair—confirms that 'Buster' could never measure up:

Two little shoes and a heart to grieve
These are the feales in fief I take,
'Til over these eyes the mists shall weave,
And my darling greets me to peace, as I wake.

———

MY MOTHER'S DEFENCE OF my father's misdemeanours was to always return to the sadness of his early years, saying, 'he had such a terrible childhood, he never experienced a normal family life, he had no example of how to be a father'. For all of that truth, he succeeded in being greatly loved by his daughters. And the best thing is: he knew it. His visit to the States, living for some weeks with Miki's family, was a cherished time. Miki wrote, after he returned to Australia, that his visit was '*a wonder and a joy*' and headed that letter: '*1974 will henceforth be known as THE YEAR DAD CAME TO VISIT.*' Distances—between countries, ages and circumstances—melted away.

I was twenty-six-years-old before I got to know Miki, my eldest sister with a heart as big as her beloved Mount Baldy, the mountain that lay beyond the orange orchards of her California home, a home I was welcomed into as though I'd been born there. In the year I lived in California, she showed me the land she loved: the redwood forests, the rocky coastline, the flowering desert, the meadows of Yosemite and the hills of San Francisco. The sadness was the sisters were scattered: the three of us would never spend a day together. A letter written by my mother to my father while he was on his California visit reminds me of the our separation: '*[Geraldine] gets weepy at everything, your card, Darl's letter . . . she's so delightfully moist when it comes to those she wants around her and the devil take the others!'*

Although we would never all be together in one place, a few years later, when Miki visited Australia, the circle was completed with Geraldine becoming her sisterly confidante and Miki dubbing Gloria 'Mother Greatheart'. At last my father could write these words to his eldest daughter:

And this old rogue purrs to himself that, after all, in a somewhat sloppy/slapdash/unadmirable way, it has all come out the way the unabashed old sentimental romantic dreamed that a family life could be, right from his pre-pubescent days.

My father had been free to travel to California because closing in on seventy he had only just retired. He was possessed of a work ethic that would see him, at the pensionable age of sixty-five, subtracting a decade off his age on a job application for full-time proof-reader at the Government Printing Office. The fact was he looked at least a decade younger than his age and so no one thought to query his white lie. Like his father Winnie, who worked with the energy of two men, and his grandfather John, who was still taking legal cases at the age of ninety, he too embraced the labour.

When my parents came to visit London in the early 1980s, my husband and I took them on a tour through France. I have never forgotten my father's lack of interest in the journey from north to south. Although he seemed vaguely taken with the lovely old towns we stayed in, as we travelled through the land-scape he was more engrossed in the book he was reading, rarely casting a glance out the car window. While it frustrated me then, I now think that he had seen all he wanted of the world. He was content. He had written a few years earlier:

I smile and laugh a lot and generally go about with a wonderful glow of well-being—happy in living and some-times with a guilt feeling that no one has the right to feel so happy, having done so little to deserve it when measured by the yardstick of general public assessment.

My mother once said that my father was envious of only one thing: Frank Sinatra's musical phrasing. I'm not even sure that was so. He was too big a man for envy and, besides, he had found what he needed. Writing to Miki he said: '*When things won't go right . . . a woman's tender understanding at such times is the greatest reward in life.*'

In most instances, he would be honest to a fault, tactless even: certainly you would never be left in doubt about his opinion, for instance: 'Do you like my new hat, Dad?' 'No, it's ridiculous.' However, he was capable of turning that directness on himself, once writing to Miki:

I've tasted nearly everything save wealth (but have moved through it, once or twice) . . . I am often flabbergasted in moments of retrospection, to see things I once thought were priorities, the expectations I had that because I saw things

as being right, or conversely of no consequence, they must
be . . . I have much to be forgiven, though, as well, much to
forgive. Hardest to accept is the former.

There was a steel core of courage in my father, certainly in his determination to speak up for what he believed to be right, and also in his silence when suffering pain. But now I believe there was even more strength to that silence. Looking back I realise that I never heard a whisper of regret about the life he had given up . . . that big public life—full of money and adulation and fame. My sister heard a murmur, just once, when she asked him to check her application form for Columbia University. Having marked up corrections, he handed the paper back with the comment: 'There was a time when I was a lot more than a proof-reader.'

Among my father's fine qualities, I put compassion highest on the list. I see it through the blur of an early photograph, taken when he is about three years old, in which he tenderly cradles a cat over half his size, his sweet face burrowing into its fur.

An image of that boy, grown to a man, comes with a backdrop of a blue Sydney sky. He carries a heavy wooden ladder that stretches two-storeys high and props it precariously against the trunk of a tall palm growing in the front garden of Bland Street, Ashfield. Then he begins to climb to the top of the tree. It's a dangerous manoeuvre, particularly as he uses just one hand to pull himself up each rung. His one-handed climb is a necessity, for in the other hand he cradles a fallen bird's egg he is returning to its nest.

In another image he is set against the dusk of a winter evening, sitting in a high-backed armchair, lamplight pooling around him. He is holding my porcelain blonde-haired doll Betty, who refuses to open her eyes. To my horror I see he has removed part of her head and with his screwdriver is poking about inside her brain; I am distraught and run from the room. But he finds me and calms me: not by arguing that my doll isn't real, but by patiently explaining she feels no pain and that soon she will flutter her beautiful eyelids once again.

Chapter Nineteen

'I F YOU HADN'T HAD the jump, you wouldn't have to hop it.'
The line runs above a large drawing of a kangaroo, and in
its pouch sits a small removable notebook containing farewell
messages from colleagues in my London ad agency presented to
me as I left my job, heavily pregnant, about to give birth to my
first child.

I discovered it recently among the paraphernalia of my own
tea chest, which comes in the shape of many large boxes. They
remind me that the past is another country or, in my case, many.
These boxes store the higgledy-piggledy of years: photographs
and letters, alongside drawings by my children, their school
reports and projects; all sorts of remembrances, things I find
impossible to throw away.

They spark trickle-down memories: the sapling gum in the
front of my first house, a minute Victorian terrace in Melbourne's
North Carlton, built where forests belonging to the Wurundjeri

peoples once flourished; my children's toy wombat in the window seat looking out on the spring green of London's Wimbledon Common, and Rupert, the black labrador, running through the white snow there, where residents once hung their washing; my sister marrying beside the long row of lavender in France's Tourrettes-sur-Loup and my mother pruning that same hedge, growing on the rise of a stone terrace where monks once cultivated bees; my daughter cutting her twenty-first birthday cake under the ceiling of New York's Dakota building, whose high beams and floorboards contain insulating soil from Central Park, where sheep once roamed; and my son, playing the didgeridoo in an attic room under the roof of Albany in Piccadilly, a place where Byron once listened to the song of his exotic birds.

Will my children, in decades to come, find themselves digging through these boxes trying to piece the past together? Did my father have this thought as he threw everything into his tea chest, like a huge stockpot to be reduced to its essence: the lessons learned, the losses shouldered, the friends made, the work achieved, the causes fought, the people cherished.

Pass it on, I think I hear him say.

Reading his words, when he describes growing old, and then realising I am older than he was when he wrote them, is like hearing a mournful cello chord. I grieve for us both.

Visiting the places my father once lived had the same melancholic effect. In 2017, I travelled to California to walk in those towns and search for traces of what my father and my American family had experienced, what they had seen. Little was left behind but nostalgia.

In Sacramento, a car park had taken the place of my grand-father Winnie's clapboard house and the garden with the cherry trees. The family home in Fullerton of my great-grandparents, Blanche and John, had disappeared under a block of flats. The Smith orchard, along with other farms surrounding the town, had long since been divided into housing lots. Bulldozed, built over, obliterated.

But Santa Maria was the epicentre for destruction. In my father's birth year of 1907, the city was shiny new—just thirty-two years old. It was self-sufficient, blessed with warmth and water. Four major ranchers had contributed a square mile each to create the town. The roads, lined with gas lamps, were named for the trees that defined them: Pine Street, Cypress Street. At night, thick fog rolled in from the coast, so thick it wet your face as it wove through the branches of trees, draping the streets in lacy silk. By day, the clapboard houses, built on wide grass-carpeted lots with porches decorated with curlicues of flowering vines, shone in bright colours. Surrounding the town, the land was so fertile it looked like a giant picnic cloth covered in all the good food the earth could produce. It was storybook perfect.

Back in that other time, the rare automobile announced itself long before it arrived, creating a small dust storm on the unpaved roads. Citizens stopped to set their watches by the great clock at the parade-wide crossroads of Broadway and Main, and the town turned on the click of leather shoes and iron horseshoes. Spires and towers flagged various places of worship, but the population was even more diverse—Spanish American, British, Scottish, Irish, Japanese, Swiss, Italian and Portuguese. Many of these families owned farms and ranches, while names like Goblentz and Schwabacher, Fleisher and Loustalot hanging over main street stores further added to the mix.

But, like a shiver of sharks, oil wells began slowly circling the town. They heralded a change that would bring shopping malls and car parks. My grandfather Winnie, witnessing the early destruction, began despairing back in the 1930s, renaming the country 'The United Oil States of America'.

I first saw Santa Maria in 1974, when my father flew from Sydney to visit his daughters—me, working in Los Angeles, and Miki, raising her family in Claremont. This was the first time he had held his eldest daughter since she was a toddler, the first time he had set eyes on his three grandchildren, and the first time he had set foot in his hometown for forty years. As our car completed its ten-mile journey from Guadalupe on Highway 101 and turned into the main street of Santa Maria, he searched in vain for something he recognised—the old family stores with their names painted on wooden signs, the tall gum trees. 'Damn the city fathers!' he exclaimed in disbelief at the impersonal neon-lit desert of concrete. 'Oh, God,' he sighed as we pulled up at the address where his grandparents' wooden house had once stood, joyful in its yellow paint. He found it replaced by a nonentity of a shack—its thirty-metre frontage, its four giant spreading pepper trees he once loved to climb, its rose garden, its barn with the hayloft—gone. 'Oh, Brother!' he bellowed, as a quick scan of his old street from corner to corner revealed not a tree left standing. And by the time I re-visited it seemed bleaker still. The Santa Maria that he remembered as 'lively, spirited, culture-loving, intriguing, cosmopolitan', had transformed into 'an unadorned, unimaginative market place'.

I am relieved my parents never returned to Stanwell Park. It would have been impossible for them to retrace their steps through the guttered streets. When I first set out on my explorations, I searched for our rented house in Fairweather Road, Bellevue Hill, and the modest brick bungalow was still standing more or less as it had in my memory. The front garden was still lush and the built-in veranda that formed the sunroom was still in place. Two years into writing this book I returned, intending to ask the owners if I might look through the house. I arrived to find a builder's truck craning breezeblocks into a vacant space where the house had been. The footings forecast that, like the majority of the new buildings springing up in the Eastern Suburbs of Sydney, the garden would be buried under maximum square metres of concrete. Sometimes I think Sydney's love of the wrecking ball means one day the only inner-city gardens of any scope will be public and nothing will be left of our history other than sepia photographs.

Photographs are all that remain of my parents' home at 35 Seaview Avenue, Newport, where they lived for the last fifteen years of their marriage after my father retired. In the years following my father's death, it became a bastion for my mother against a thieving disease. I will never return to that address for I am told three separate villas now stand in the place of that almost century-old weatherboard named 'Banksia', one of the first houses built in the area, with its corrugated iron roof, high brick chimney and sprawling garden. To keep company with the gnarly grove of trees that gave the house its name, my sister and I planted iron-barks, spotted gums and red gums that all grew to glorious maturity. The trees, home to Mrs Possum and her brood—gone. The window seat and the spare bedroom, the occasional home to Mr and Mrs Possum—gone. The love ploughed under.

But the children who played in their grandparents' house will remember that garden: my daughter Cassie, who flew on the swing my father, her 'Da', had strung over a low-hanging tree branch; or her brother Sam, who sat in his wading pool and watched his grandmother mix flour, water and cochineal, and shape cakes to bake on the big hot sandstone rocks; or my sister's son, Nathaniel, who, imagining himself a wizard, leapt and hid and charged about the green place, adventuring until the sun went down.

———

I GREW UP LISTENING to my father sing. I'd hear him rehearsing in the bedroom, preparing for concerts or recording sessions, running through his chords, tapping his tuning fork to find the notes and cupping his ear to judge if he was pitch perfect. He'd sing as we washed and dried the dishes together. He'd sing all about the house. His voice was part of my every day.

But on the second last Christmas before his death, I was jolted into understanding that his voice was way out of the way of the every day. That Christmas he summoned strength to come to the table in his pyjamas and dressing gown for our celebratory dinner. Afterwards, we all sang carols and I asked him to sing our favourite, as he had for almost every Christmas I could remember. Despite his lungs being weakened by emphysema, he agreed.

I wasn't expecting to hear anything like the strength of his old range, but suddenly I worried that he might not be able to reach the high notes. But then his lyrical voice rose feather light on 'silent night', streamed clear through the air with 'holy night' and continued on in graceful loops and bends, until finally soaring to the pure clear height of 'heavenly peace' before making the deep descent back to earth.

As the room filled with applause, I remember his face—the pleasure it showed at the pleasure he had given. He'd cracked the ceiling with his song and, for a brief moment, the old weatherboard had become a cathedral. It was a late revelation and it was at that moment I realised my father, like a great poet or painter, had the power to transform.

—

I BELIEVE THE ONLY time I heard my mother talk of her mortality was when she said: 'To die of cancer would be a terrible death.' She was spared that. Instead she was destined, for over a decade and a half, to take a lonely journey out of this world through a maze mapped by Alzheimer's. In this labyrinth she struggled, becoming more and more confused and anxious, and ultimately completely lost amid the tangles of dead-ends and signs that misted over before she could reach them.

It began slowly: confusing messages, forgetting names, finding it difficult to negotiate new places. For some time, we simply put it down to forgetfulness. Immediately after our father died, my sister and I vied competitively for her to live with one or the other of us, with me in the UK or Geraldine in the USA, but she steadfastly refused us both. Even then I think she couldn't consider leaving the security of her home. As time progressed, she became more and more reluctant to venture out, other than a daily trip to local shops that she could still easily negotiate. Her home was comfortingly familiar and filled with prompts—flowers she'd planted, machines she could manipulate, photographs and objects she recognised. It was a place she could live with a degree of autonomy. While she could my sister and I did all we could to keep her there.

There was the added benefit that people kept a kindly eye on her. It seemed everyone knew my mother. It was impossible to take the five-minute walk to the shops without it stretching to half an hour because of the long line of people who wanted to stop and talk. Since the year of my parents' arrival in Newport in 1978, her front-door bell had rung to the lyrics, 'Glor . . . Glor . . . Gloria, yoo hoo! . . . are you home?' She could never turn anyone away and the kettle would be put on for the umpteenth time that day. When people or ideas she held dear needed defending, she would be there, a conquistadora in a cotton frock. She was the one out in the streets selling raffle tickets to save the Franklin River. She was the one thrusting leaflets into people's hands, urging them to save the ABC. She was the one standing in the pouring rain outside the Newport Surf Club handing out tickets to vote for the Republic. And, she was the one rushing from the pharmacy with a sunhat quickly purchased for the baby she saw distressed under a hot summer sun.

For years she could play cards, write short letters, follow knitting patterns and, up to the last year of her life, remember old song lyrics; but one of the first and hardest losses to witness was her reading. I'd watch her at breakfast, stuck on the front page of the paper, returning and returning to the same early paragraphs of an article as she laboured to keep the storyline in her head.

And for years she seemed, while in the moment, to be her old self and our conversations would flow as they always had—funny, intimate, comforting. But, seeking her valued counsel increasingly became a vain hope. Despite believing an important subject had registered, when I revisited the issue, not even a nugget remained. All that we had spoken of previously was gone, erased.

Her wonderful wit, her word play, slowly became more and more cryptic like her crosswords—but they were among the last things lost. Forgetting names and places, she would greet people with flattery and questions: 'Hello, you attractive man' or 'Good to see you, you beautiful girl' or 'Now tell me, when was it we last met?'

Before the disease really took hold, Geraldine or I would arrange for her to be escorted through airports and she would stay with one or the other of us. Once, while with me in New York City, she surprised me with her memory. She had asked why small groups gathered outside every day with flowers, gazing up at our apartment building. Not expecting her to remember,

I explained John Lennon had once lived in the place and his followers were waiting for a glimpse of his widow. As days went by, I noticed her habit of standing by one of the tall windows while knitting; when I saw her waving, I asked if she had recognised someone on 72nd Street. 'Oh no, Darl, I just didn't want to disappoint all those people. I wave and they wave back, and then they go away happy.' I wonder now how many people in Japan are holding photographs and pointing to my mother in the window of the fifth floor of the Dakota and calling her Yoko.

As she struggled to find the right words, she could be uniquely descriptive. To my son Sam, who at the time was darkly bearded, she instructed: 'Get that dirt off your handsome face, pet.' And if she missed nuances, she still listened in. While shopping together, she overheard my request to the salesperson for postcards of Martha's Vineyard. In a fed-up tone she enquired: '*Who* is this woman everyone is *always* talking about?'

Constantly trying to reel her back into the present, while travelling on a ferry journey I asked her where we were. She thought for a moment and then, with a tilt of her head and a cheeky smile, she replied: 'I'm where you are.' Next, I asked her to look out the window and tell me what she saw, hoping for the pedantic response of 'water'. Instead, with wave-like motions of her hand, she murmured: 'Going . . . going . . .'

When she no longer recognised her home, but before she needed round-the-clock carers, she went to live with Geraldine on the island of Martha's Vineyard. There were illnesses and accidents. After flying out from Sydney to be by her side on one such emergency, my brother-in-law Tony picked me up from the ferry dock and whisked me to the hospital where my mother lay with a broken hip. We entered the room and she beamed at Tony, lavishing him with a fulsome greeting, but ignoring me. Having immediately jumped onto a plane and flown for twenty hours, made a long car journey and a ferry trip, I stood there not only exhausted but deflated. Suddenly her eyes changed focus and pointing across the room in my direction, she exclaimed: 'I know *you*—you're me!'

Among family papers, I found a letter not sent that had been written by my mother. With the disease beginning to blur her memory, there is every chance she forgot to post it simply because she had forgotten she wrote it. Dated February 1999, it is addressed to the editor of the *Sydney Morning Herald*:

Dear Sir,

I grew up in the depression days and after school I would listen to the radio (or the 'wireless' as I called it), mostly the ABC.

My parents were out working, or busy elsewhere, so the little I knew about life was from the beautiful voices coming from the ABC and they taught me how to speak correctly (I still listen every day).

Later in life I had no trouble getting a job on 2GB and 2CA as a radio announcer myself. You can see then why I love the Australian Broadcasting Commission.

Hands off please, Senator Alston!

By the time she composed that letter, she had been widowed for five years.

My father was ill many years before his death. Throughout that time, every January when I returned to London, I dreaded kissing him goodbye, always feeling it might be our last embrace. Each Christmas the signs of his increasing infirmity multiplied: from handrails to plastic chairs in the shower, to nurses and physios visiting daily, to the necessity of a huge industrial-type mixer grinding away a blend of vegetables and vitamins to sustain him as his weakening body rejected solids. In his final bedridden year, my mother nursed him obsessively. Although still possessed of his scalpel-sharp mind, as his emphysema worsened and began to block oxygen, he would have brief hallucinatory spells that never allowed my mother an ordered day, or a full night's rest. The result was a warning to her from the family doctor: 'You'll go before your husband if you keep this up.'

At Christmas in 1993, I was shocked to see her. Never weighing more than 45 kilos, she had become skeletal. Her whole being was so devoted to the care of her husband that not even her grandchildren could distract her that summer. However, she was exhausted enough to agree to my father being admitted to a Dee Why hospital for a fortnight while she recuperated and regained some weight and strength. During that time, I did my utmost to convince her to visit care facilities in the area, and in my rented car we searched for a suitable place that would be easily reachable for her daily by public transport.

Before she had to make the dreaded but inevitable decision that January, one morning the phone rang as a blazing hot day dawned. I knew it was a call from the hospital long before I heard her crippled voice tell me, 'Daddy died.' My first reaction wasn't grief—it was relief. That is a terrible admission, compounded by the fact that I had orchestrated his time in hospital, robbing my mother of the thing she wanted so dearly: 'A man should be able to die in his own home.'

Now I question whether, if I had been living in Sydney, perhaps I wouldn't have been in such a rush to change the situation. Instead, I would have been on hand to help out on a daily basis. During his stay in the hospital, my father had been moved from a lovely sunny aspect on the ground floor, to a dingy basement-level room with a small window and a subterranean view. On one of our last visits he had reiterated his need for a physio, and I didn't follow up my mother's request to the nurses to ensure that this happened. One redeeming hope remains: if my father had been in full control of his rational self, he wouldn't have wanted the life my mother was so insistent he cling to.

Her grief in the hospital that morning was overwhelmingly raw, so devastatingly private, it forced my eyes to the floor. As we entered that room, she cried out and in a second she was next to him, feeling his face, her hands running along his body, clutching at him, oblivious to the world as she cried: 'Oh, no, oh, no, he's warm . . . he's still warm!' Her voice shattering in disbelief. 'It can't have been long since . . .' I wonder now if he died in the same hour as his father. I remember him telling me that Winnie had passed away at 4 a.m., saying it was the time when the body was at its lowest ebb.

Looking at his wasted body, his sunken face, his mouth frozen in the shape of his desperate last breath, I was reminded of the shell of a cicada and I was comforted that he had flown. I felt his presence in that room—removed, but above us. For around a year after, in the quiet of the night, I would sometimes have a positive sense of his energy circling, further and further away as time went on. It is the one and only time in my life I have felt anything vaguely mystical. I didn't experience it at the deathbed of my mother. She left us slowly and, at a certain point within the last cruel six months of her life, she appeared to have gone completely.

Unlike my mother, my father often referred to death, but only in the most positive of ways. He had lost his fear of it early in life and it had never returned. He had, in one of his numerous letters to journalist Phillip Adams, boasted as much, with Adams blithely countering: *'I know a couple of people who insist that they have no anxiety about death . . . I can assure you that the sudden appearance of a fourteen-foot homicidal maniac from Venezuela would rekindle that suppressed fear.'* But Adams had no idea of the brave heart encased in the 1.68-metre frame of Lawrie Brooks—he would have stood his ground and faced down that Venezuelan.

Part of my father's agnostic belief was that if we learned to harvest the huge percentage of our brains left languishing, we might communicate telepathically and perhaps discover other realms in space and time. I believe he saw death as a possible adventure—and, if not, he was content with the one he was living. He wrote to Miki: *'Why worry about the "who" created*

*it all? We are given one capacity that makes it all worthwhile—
the capacity to love. Genuine, sharing, unselfish, helpful love
is the answer to all progress.'*

While my mother usually accompanied her children to
Sunday Mass, and my father appreciated a well-tuned hymn,
religion or the afterlife was not a subject of discussion in our
house. But the liturgy of their hours rang consistently and,
despite troubles and arguments, they kept the faith that they
would always be together.

———

AMONG THE MANY PHOTOGRAPHS in the tea chest were pictures
commissioned by my mother in her role as Publicity Officer.
In one photograph taken at South Head, my father poses with
his jacket slung over his shoulder, while his other arm is flung
around a female singer. In another, my mother (newly married)
joins my father in a line-up of musicians and comedians from the
Entertainment Unit: linked arm in arm, they kick the foam along
the shoreline of Bondi Beach for the publicity photographer.

The most surprising of all my discoveries was a thin sheet of
paper, lost amid a jumble of documents I had boxed up while
clearing out the Newport house. I almost threw it away, but just
in time noticed a faint pencil imprint in my mother's hand. It's
too late to ask if she was the poet, but the litany of places they
had lived and travelled through, suggests she was. I believe this
message to my father that he never read contains the answer to
the question that puzzled me from the beginning: why was a
stage life exchanged for a suburban world? And it seems fitting

that Gloria—the maestro, the conductor of all our lives—finally explains the equation. It is as simple as it is complicated. It had been the means by which a man contrived to stay with a woman, in a place they both called home.

I do not need, tis very true
To dedicate my poems to you
Since, in a way, you made them too
Through all the years and in all the weather
We've climbed the hills and tramped together
Past Coogee and Centennial Park
Past Bronte, Manly, Bulli Pass
From Palm Beach through the Forest French
To Bondi, Nielsen and the rest
We've sheltered from the bitter winds
And cracked our jokes and left behind
Our footsteps threading through the grass
Our voices talking down the pass
So when at last I ope my eyes
On other scenes beyond the skies
If this, indeed, is Heaven I'll say
Where are the coves and Watson's Bay?
Where the long line of South Head too?
And where, I ask, where are you?

Afterword

I HAD HOPED BY DIGGING through the tea chest I would find my father.

I found little pieces of him in articles, photographs, letters and the cat's cradle of memory. They were like shards of coloured glass that, when clustered together and held to the light, fell into a fleeting image of him. But then, with the smallest tilt of reflection, of point of view, he shifted again and reformed.

Yet the image of him reading *Alice in Wonderland* to me, night after night, continuing on faithfully through the chapters— that remains fixed.

And now it feels as though he has always been reading it to me, reading on until I finally come to understand what the Mad Hatter had so sanely recognised—time can't be frozen. And just like the White Rabbit, I was destined from the very beginning to always be late. To be running forever after that sweet man, my father, back through time in a vain effort to catch him.

Acknowledgements

WITHOUT THE ENCOURAGEMENT OF my sister Geraldine, I would not have attempted this book. Without the support of my husband, Geoffrey Cousins, I would not have completed it. And without the guidance of Richard Walsh, it would not have reached the light.

Thanks to Dean Thomas who planted the seed, and to my readers: Geraldine Brooks, Geoffrey Cousins, Sam Bungey, Cassie Bungey, Michael Bungey, Nathaniel Brooks-Horwitz, Erik Eklöf, Jacki Lyden, Alison Hulett, Graham Thorburn, Juliet Ashworth and Christina Kennedy. I am indebted to Edward Bratt, my nephew, who so diligently archived family letters, to my niece Renata Bratt for her kind help and my stalwart publisher, Rebecca Kaiser. But above all, my gratitude to Miki, whose correspondence between herself and our father has formed the spine of this book. All together under the same roof at last.

Sources

An Entertaining War, Michael Pate, Dreamweaver Books, Sydney, 1986

Hollywood, Mayfair and all that Jazz: The Roy Fox story, Leslie Frewin, London, 1975

Peter Finch: A biography, Trader Faulkner, Angus & Robertson, UK, 1979

A Showman's Story: The memoirs of Jim Davidson, Rigby, Adelaide, 1983

Wonderful Wireless: Reminiscences of the stars of Australia's live radio, Nancye Bridges, Methuen, Sydney, 1983

Access to archives of Ed Bratt, California: letters between Miki Bratt and Lawrie Brooks, Katharine Smith and Robert Cutter, Louise Conkey and Blanche Conkey

Access to archives of Renata Bratt

Access to archives of Geraldine Brooks

Article by Gloria Brooks celebrating Australian radio

Interviews with Geraldine Brooks

Interview with Tony Horwitz

Interview with Harry Griffiths

Letter from Leslie Smith describing Smith ranch

Short story written by Lawrie Brooks (depicting character of Gloria van Boss)

A
Poem
for
Record
Keepers

ARGOS
BOOKS

A
Poem
for
Record
Keepers

Ali
Power

Grateful acknowledgement to the editors of the following publications where some of these poems originally appeared:

Bort Quarterly: 22, 23, 24, 25, 26, 27, 28
The Brooklyn Rail: 2, 5, 7, 9, 11, 12, 16, 17, 18, 19, 20, 21, 31, 32, 33, 34, 37, 42, 43, 44, 46, 48, 49
LIT: 10, 14, 29, 38, 40, 45
The PEN Poetry Series: 1, 3, 4, 8, 13, 15, 36

ISBN: 978-1-938247-25-5
Library of Congress Control Number: 2016900122

Cover art: Based on cyanotype from the collection *Photographs of British Algae* by Anna Atkins

Book design by Mårten Wessel

First printing: March 2016

Argos Books
www.argosbooks.org

Contents

A Poem for Record Keepers

I must unlearn what has been taught me.

—John Wieners

I

Like love is embarrassing.

—Michael Gizzi

(1)

Dylan didn't write all the lyrics on *Desire*.

You ask what makes a poem.

The sun makes you sneeze.

Another coattail descends extraordinary stairs.

Put them in order.

Put them on top of me.

I am perfecting my organs.

(2)

Neil Young used to dig Picasso.

Memory inherits paralysis.

I'm all fucked up on feeling(s).

Can I count on you?

Tugboat.

The sea is immense.

Drink up.

(3)

Once there were three kinds of being(s).

7 1 1 1 6 2 6.

Sometimes I write down a series of numbers.

Can I make the garden grow?

"You're doing a beautiful job."

Like oars.

There's a postcard coming from Exactly What I Mean.

(4)

Someday we'll oppose each other in the championship game.

Old women of Sunday.

February on the houses.

Still another delicate head.

You were looking at everyone.

But you wanted everyone to look at you.

Hurry up.

(5)

It's necessary that everyone can have something.

Italian sub.

Dictionary.

A general dullness.

(Being versus appearing.

Gray.)

Almost snow.

(6)

People who can build toilets are capable of anything.

You move from one shit show to the next.

A cartography of public restrooms.

I stick around.

Weigh things and make them equal.

Chin up.

A heart isn't something you just have.

(7)

Reading used to mean fortune telling.

I want to remember every song.

But what I wanted before I don't want anymore.

Because I'm getting something else instead.

My name is Babe.

I sell perfume.

Thank you for your order.

||

sun is rising / it has risen / there is radio

—Simone Kearney

(8)

There is GPS.

There is Florida.

There is pinecone.

There is trampoline.

There is olive oil.

There is getting to know you.

There is never getting to know all about you.

(9)

Henry Hudson captained the Half Moon in 1608.

Today people die because they don't know where they're going.

Fung Wah feathers.

Call back my half.

"[B]ecause we were sliced like filets of sole."

Hopping on one leg.

Go go.

(10)

I'm no longer interested in how my parents fucked me up.

The truth is not.

Decorative pillows.

Painted explanations.

Go in and out.

Go slow.

We are not cars.

(11)

We are not baseball.

Don't hold me responsible.

Eyelid of idiocy.

Daughter of drug flutter.

I know what's good.

There is soup.

Try it.

(12)

Davy Crockett at the Academy.

MOBY DICK when I sit.

What's a name?

John Paul Jones.

Yellow houses of holes.

Take me by.

The port's mouth.

(13)

"Cut your losses," said the Viking.

This is supposed to be fun.

But then your neighbor & her friend invite themselves in.

Ask if we're having a party (are terrible dancers).

Improvisers in mirage.

They whistle.

Write that down.

(14)

We were all having fun.

We were getting used to it.

Then too many French phrases.

Too many breasts.

We are not figurative.

We are not pom-poms.

Woah-oh.

III

Sadness leaves the body dumb.

—Claire Donato

(15)

Don't be so dumb.

Offspring of autobiography.

Asking for sex.

After we get books we'll get accents.

Behave badly.

In blouses.

Before boarding the atmosphere.

(16)

I don't trust men with hairless chests.

Get serious.

Wet your face before getting indigestion.

Before ordering huevos rancheros.

Picture tree surgeons on the tops of New Jersey.

Singing.

Get on with your life.

(17)

When Robert Plant sings.

"Wanna Whole Lotta Love."

He's talking about suffering.

Give the people what they want.

Turn / turn back / turn away / turn on.

Covered / uncovered / naked / not naked.

How do you make your music?

(18)

A pamphlet, a manifesto, an instruction manual.

You'd rather be a fortune-teller.

A navigator.

A projector.

You want to sing.

You contain, you know.

Do you know?

III

(19)

Scientists study deception.

At the front desk.

A vague politeness.

But let's keep talking.

I'm so well-equipped.

In unbearable situations.

It's my one virtue.

(20)

Chicken wings.

With a side of stuff.

Sincerity.

Or the new insincerity.

I'm sorry.

The moon used to be closer to the earth.

Remember / time?

(21)

Socrates used to say, "What do you want?"

In fancy sandals.

In the vertiginous lost & found.

We are codenames.

We are irregular patches of dust.

Phosphorescent swarms of ellipses in the afternoon.

Return to our jobs.

IV

Let's hang out.

—Anonymous

(22)

Sometimes when I eat I feel like I'm suffering.

It forms along the edges.

Of bad readings and baggage claims.

A longitudinal swirl of pearl-pins on the hems.

Of my lineage.

You like my ass.

Let's hang out.

(23)

Are you the type of person who knows things?

Do you wonder what children do?

There's an omelet on your chest.

There are rivers and oceans still hiding.

There are flowers.

All the dinosaurs are dead.

Let's hang out.

(24)

Studies gauge the effects of divorce on children.

There is nowhere, but we have commas.

Count them at breakfast.

Unfold / refolding / print.

"I wish there was a war."

Alexander Hamilton wrote in 1769.

Let's hang out.

(25)

As you drop into it you call it darkness.

It's talking too much.

Its smoothness carries you.

Toward on and on . . . and on.

And so on.

Blah blah.

Let's hang out.

(26)

Everything is just beginning.

Everything is comprehensible.

Take, for example, Utah.

Until you break it down.

It's like that proverb says.

I'm so fucking bored.

Let's hang out.

(27)

My head's on a loop, large and/or.

I can't tell.

Its ecstatic circumference unknown.

Like a fire's spreading in the cosmos.

Enabling its condition I laugh when shit becomes too much.

But more.

Let's hang out.

(28)

Don't take it personally.

Your personal abyss.

I don't understand the meaning of equilibrium.

Or the anamorphousness of our selves, say.

"I know exactly what you mean."

I will fuck up your life.

Let's hang out.

V

I am just coming / Just going in

—Joseph Ceravolo

(29)

I need less and less attention.

As we pass through uneven tufts of pastoral pornography.

I am no longer so pale.

My paleness no longer grows.

Overnight.

It softens.

The seasons are still coming; the seasons keep coming one by one.

(30)

Later, on the reified Ikea odyssey.

Certain conditions sink deeper and deeper.

Under our very eyes.

There's no need that can't increase.

Examine both sides of this machine.

The rising ever-rising jerk.

The happiness of all, etc.

(31)

Spring song.

So many ugly hats.

Dismembered cloud transmissions.

From exiled fashion designers.

And long-deceased seamstresses.

At once swaths.

Of synthetic turf in viscous folds.

(32)

Dante died in transit.

Keats in Rome.

Pound, Venice; Montale, Milan.

Orgy of want.

Vestibule of don't want.

I'm trying to locate the shiny spot.

On your glass.

(33)

You want a location.

But you really mean a telescope.

I hand you the champagne from no occasion.

Should I keep going?

In certain rooms we can only look ahead.

Looking ahead is fun.

When you're delusional.

(34)

Shuttlecock is shortened to shuttle.

Shuffle the shuttle of the loom.

The cock part (made of feathers).

Breaks easily, is replaced with plastic.

I find the hardest part.

About talking.

Is the part about talking.

(35)

Sometimes we say things we don't mean.

Sometimes we say things we do mean but then say, "I didn't mean it."

Because what was said was mean.

And the truth hurts.

I find comfort in knowing when to use a comma.

It gives me a sense of certainty in this uncertain world.

This is my trousseau, my love.

VI

I didn't know whether to jerk off or to kill somebody

—Clark Coolidge

(36)

"Why does someone have to die?"

Sportscasters and academics are all alike.

They know what they're saying.

But they're not saying anything.

Disaster-piece theater.

In the diabetic sock section.

I wrote this for you.

(37)

Every day we find new ways to insult each other.

The sudden we.

Miscalculating the myriad of Mary-Anns tights-less in Florida.

"Make something / do something to it / do something to that."

Delete.

Delete.

Delete.

(38)

We give each other names.

It feels good.

We heal well.

And often.

How much distance are you supposed to keep between yourself and others?

In line.

At the pharmacy.

(39)

There are no prizes.

In Canada.

You stick out your tongue.

In the hotel parking lot.

It tastes like sex.

What's the name you called me at the imagined biennale?

I never quite learned how to take a compliment.

(40)

If I can't have one.

And you can't have one.

And if you won't give me one.

Then you can't have yours.

But it's still the same question.

The same feeling.

Keep the tacos coming.

(41)

Looking at the sky feels good.

Do you need an explanation?

Blue is the color of the mind.

Blue is the world's favorite color.

Meanwhile, we're basking in the negative capability.

Of business casual.

There are no windows here.

(42)

I'm beginning to wonder if this is just a coping mechanism.

A way to move the space between ideas and things.

A strange community of nets.

Never ending free-throws.

But sometimes I can feel calm.

Like right now.

Because tonight we'll watch the Spurs & the Heat & touch each other.

VII

You wanna get married?

—Bernadette Mayer

(43)

Was it curiosity or boredom that brought us here?

I ask because it's summer.

And we're always reorganizing our dreams.

A glistening ecosystem of Dairy Queens.

Taut cones.

Not all women age so gracefully.

Hurry home.

(44)

Branches become mythologies.

Satellites broadcasting our mutual solitudes.

We cover a lot of miles.

Then unpack immediately.

We make a great team.

At the town fair.

I cover the sun with a steel cloak.

(45)

How we look depends on how we see.

How quickly we recover from the disappointment of ceilings.

The guided tour ends.

We get out of line.

We wait somewhere else.

I want to be in rooms that are open.

I want to be in open rooms always and with you.

(46)

The way you nod your head is comforting.

Looking up.

Waving red garments.

Ancient fireworks.

It's going through the spectrum you say as we round the bend.

We catch a glimpse of the stationary.

We give sensations names.

(47)

The way comes to an end.

We don't always win.

Crossing nascent football fields.

We share moans over the loudspeaker.

Over the hypnotic headbands of the Empire State.

Ask the astronomer.

About his robe.

(48)

Crosby, Stills, Nash, & Young is not a good band name.

Despite what you think.

I'm not that girl.

I never lie, but.

I'm still learning how to tell the truth.

I'm still practicing kissing.

Call it "Studying Hunger."

(49)

Speaking is translating.

Words have specific uses.

Like fingers.

We make lists while constellations shift over Texas.

Transmissions of our likeness.

We are glowing.

Hold your applause.